Language Planning as a Sociolinguistic Experiment

Language Planning as a Sociolinguistic Experiment

The Case of Modern Norwegian

Ernst Håkon Jahr

EDINBURGH
University Press

© Ernst Håkon Jahr, 2014

Edinburgh University Press Ltd
The Tun - Holyrood Road, 12 (2f) Jackson's Entry, Edinburgh EH8 8PJ

www.euppublishing.com

Typeset in 11/13 Ehrhardt MT by
Servis Filmsetting Ltd, Stockport, Cheshire,
and printed and bound in Great Britain by
CPI Group (UK) Ltd, Croydon CR0 4YY

A CIP record for this book is available from the British Library

ISBN 978 0 7486 3782 9 (hardback)
ISBN 978 0 7486 7834 1 (webready PDF)

Contents

List of figures

Preface

This book presents the main results of my research and work on Norwegian language planning and language conflict – carried out over more than four decades from the early 1970s to the present day. The Norwegian case offers an excellent opportunity to study in detail the complicated interplay between social class and language planning against the background of general political developments. My intention here is to describe this interplay and, by doing so, convey a coherent overview of and insights into the development of Norwegian language planning.

Any generalising begs further discussion. At the same time, we have to generalise in order to be able to present potent models of explanation. My presentation herein will certainly meet with objections and alternative views. Or, at least, I hope it will. Research on modern Norwegian language history has mostly involved empirical work, and a great deal of important data and various materials have been collected over the years; however, there have been fewer overall analyses and contributions leading to deeper insights into the social and political motivations and driving forces of Norwegian language planning. In quite a number of earlier accounts, the sociolinguistic experiment which was salient in the 1938 reform has often been difficult to observe because it was concealed in the presentation of too much data.

In this book, I try to delineate the long paths of language planning in Norway. In order to do so, a broad brush was necessary, and a great many details, interesting enough in themselves, had to be disregarded.

The amount of data in this book has thus been cut to a minimum and is included for exemplification only. If I had wanted to write a much bigger book I could have done so simply by multiplying the amount of data presented, as they are literally unlimited. Undoubtedly, that would have masked my main intention with this book: to give the reader a coherent understanding of language planning in modern Norway.

The capital of Norway, Oslo, was previously named after the Dano-Norwegian King Christian IV (1577–1648; King from 1588). Thus, in 1814 the city's name was Christiania. In 1862, the spelling of /k/ was changed from *ch* to *k*, so the name became Kristiania. Since 1 January 1925, the city has been called by its medieval name, Oslo. In this book, I use the name for the capital which was contemporary for each period, thus, first Christiania, then Kristiania, and finally Oslo. This principle also applies in the References.

I am grateful to Jean Hannah and Peter Trudgill for important and very useful comments, and am also grateful to Jean for excellent copy-editing of the whole manuscript. I also want to thank Karin Lee Hansen who advised on the English of my first draft.

Ernst Håkon Jahr
Xristos Research Centre, Lesbos, August 2013

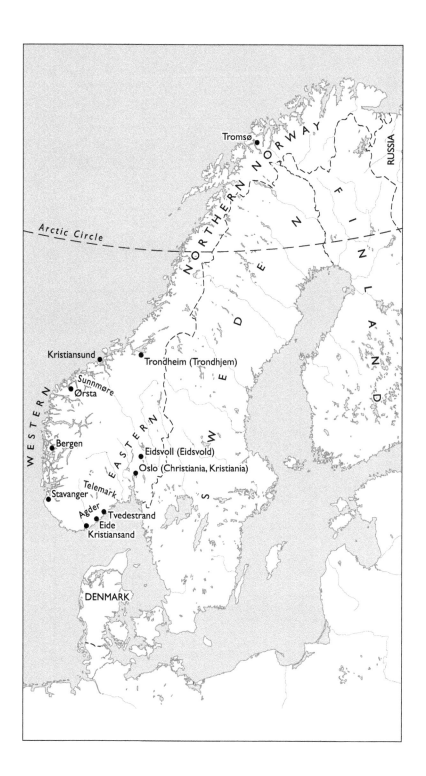

CHAPTER 1

Land and people, language and language planning

INTRODUCTION

This book is about language planning, especially its limits. How far can language planners go? How extensively can they change and/or direct the development of a given language? What are the sociolinguistic and sociopolitical boundaries within which language planning can operate and succeed? Is it possible to change the sociolinguistic pattern of a country through language planning? To what extent can language planning be a sociolinguistic and sociopolitical experiment? This book will explore these questions through an analysis of the development of modern Norwegian.

Two written Norwegian standards

Since 1885, Norway has maintained two written language standards, now known as *Bokmål* and *Nynorsk*. Through various reforms in the twentieth and twenty-first centuries – the latest having been put into effect on 1 August 2012 – these standards have moved much closer to each other linguistically. Bokmål is the majority form, and about 90 per cent of the population report that they use this standard, while 10 per cent report using Nynorsk. However, Nynorsk has a better foothold in society than the 9–1 ratio may suggest, and has its stronghold in the western part of the country.

These two standards are defined by the Language Act of 1980 as being completely equal officially. Schoolchildren are taught both; one of them is their principal standard (*hovedmål*) and the other is their secondary standard (*sidemål*). In 2013, between 12 per cent and 13 per cent of elementary-school pupils had Nynorsk as their principal standard. High-school students have had to pass exams in both of these standards since 1907.

While it is not uncommon for a country to have more than one official written language, what is unique about Norway is that this nation of just five million inhabitants maintains two different written standards *of the same language*. Moreover, there are only small linguistic differences between these two written standards, although most Norwegians recognise that the distinctions are sociolinguistically important. To many people, the use of Nynorsk or Bokmål frequently signals different values, opinions and attitudes. The reasons for this will be made clear in the following chapters.

If we compare the two written Norwegian standards to, for example, those for Swedish or Danish, another important difference soon emerges. In Swedish and Danish, there is generally only one way to write, conjugate or decline a word. There are exceptions in both languages, but as a rule there are only a few parallel forms in Swedish and Danish. This is not the case in Norwegian, which stands out as being much more diffuse in nature. For example, in both Bokmål and Nynorsk, there are many parallel and optional word forms and morphological forms for individual users to choose from. Often one can conjugate a word in several ways, or the word may belong to different morphological categories depending on the language users' choice.

How has this situation arisen in the two standards? Even if we accept that there are two written Norwegian standards, why is each of them not as invariable and specific as the Swedish and Danish standards? The simple answer is that they just are not like that, and the more detailed answer may be found in the history of the language after 1814. To complicate the situation even further, over the years both official standards have encountered competition from various private norms and standards.

The spoken language

In Sweden and Denmark, as in France and Poland, we find a standard spoken language which students are expected to learn in school (Jahr and Janicki 1995). Local dialects have a much lower social status in these countries than is the case in Norway, where pupils are allowed to use their local dialect in school. It is even stated in the current School Act that they have the right to do so. The School Act also requires teachers to respect their pupils' local dialect and not attempt to make them abandon it. The use of local dialects has on the whole a more prominent place in Norwegian schools and community life than in most other European countries.

While the language used by non-standard speakers of, for example, Hungarian, Polish or Russian may be referred to by the general public as 'bad Hungarian', 'bad Polish' or 'bad Russian', a parallel notion of 'bad Norwegian' does not exist. One cannot refer to any variety of Norwegian used by a native speaker as 'bad' and get away with it socially. Obviously, this has to do with the fact that the very concept of 'non-standard' is quite problematic and disputed in Norway. Many – perhaps a majority – of native Norwegians would deny that there is a spoken Norwegian standard. True enough, there are two official written standards, and, in addition, several unofficial private written norms or standards have emerged during almost 200 years of language planning, but this abundance of proposed and accepted written standards does not have an equivalent in standard spoken varieties. Instead, we might say that the diffuse situation when it comes to writing is reflected in the fact that there is no generally accepted spoken Norwegian standard. In fact, in Norway more people use more dialect in more situations for more purposes than in most other European countries (Trudgill 2002: 31).

In all areas of society, therefore, we find that dialects are used: in pre-school centres, schools, universities – among professors as well as among students, in the media, on television and radio, very often in private letters and electronic text messages, Internet blogs, poetry and novels, theatres and Norwegian movies, and in the workplace as well as in government and Parliament. Many government ministers always speak their local dialect, and many of them gain an increased level of popular support and trust by doing just that.

Standard Bokmål read with eastern Norwegian phonology and prosody is not infrequently referred to as 'standard eastern Norwegian' or even 'standard Norwegian'. Such sentiments are found especially in Oslo and the areas around the capital. For some people it is both difficult and frustrating that Norwegian does not offer a standard spoken variety as does Swedish, Polish and French. There is no doubt that the strongest candidate for such a spoken standard in Norway is a variety closely linked to written Bokmål spoken with an eastern accent. While there are individuals on radio and television (almost exclusively newsreaders or anchors) who normalise their speech and who follow the written standard closely with regard to word forms and morphology, be it in Bokmål or Nynorsk, they still more or less keep their original local accent intact.

This extensive use of local dialects in all walks of life and society in general is not supported officially in any special way but is nowadays seen as normal linguistic behaviour in Norway. We will examine how this situation grew out of a principle first adopted by Parliament in 1878. Early in the 1900s, the situation developed further through struggles over regulations concerning the language of instruction in schools. Starting with an important court case about language use on radio and television in the early 1960s, we can trace a direct line up to the year 2010, when the Norwegian Broadcasting Corporation (NRK) employed the first television anchorperson who read the news using a salient local (northern Norwegian) dialect.

A survey investigating attitudes towards various accents and dialects on radio and television (Kulbrandstad 2011) revealed a very liberal attitude among the entire population – and not only to local dialect use. New Norwegian ethnolects which have developed over the past few decades and which are associated with various immigrant groups were also found to be acceptable to a large degree.

Almost 200 years of language planning

In Norway, the Nynorsk standard has always been regarded by a majority of people as the odd one out, a special case, 'constructed' and 'artificial' in nature. Bokmål, on the other hand, is generally seen as the 'natural' and 'obvious' language choice. However, from a more global perspective, there is no doubt that Bokmål is the more unusual case, in part due to its special history. There is no known parallel to Bokmål in any part of the world. Nynorsk, in this broader international context, is much closer to the national standards that we find in other countries where standards have been established through language planning.

Studying Norwegian language history over the past 200 years, which takes in extensive language planning and language conflict, is the only means by which we can acquire an understanding of the current exceptional situation of both the written standard(s) and spoken Norwegian.

The year 1814: the birth of modern Norway

In Norway, 1814 was a year of important and dramatic events politically. But linguistically speaking, there was not a great deal that happened. Modern Norway came into being early that year when Denmark, which had sided with France during the Napoleonic Wars, lost control of Norway, which it had governed for several centuries, to Sweden, through Napoleon's defeat at Leipzig in 1813. Sweden had joined forces with Napoleon's enemies and thus emerged victorious.

The arrangement was that Sweden would acquire Norway from Denmark as a spoil of war. However, the Norwegians revolted against this decision. A meeting of representatives from all over the country was summoned at Eidsvold, north of Christiania, to draft and approve a constitution for Norway and to elect a king. On 17 May 1814, the representatives formally adopted their new constitution, which was the most democratic in Europe at the time, drawing extensively on principles of both the American and French Revolutions. Today, this constitution, with its later amendments, ranks as the oldest in Europe.

Sweden at the time was led by a newly elected crown prince, Carl Johan Bernadotte, since there was no obvious heir to the Swedish throne. Bernadotte, who had been one of Napoleon's generals, did not accept the Norwegians' declaration of independence and the election of their own king. A brief war followed in August 1814, during which the Norwegians were defeated by the Swedes. However, the great powers of Europe did not want Sweden to become too strong, and, with their indirect support, the Norwegians were able to salvage most of their new constitution through negotiations with the Swedes that autumn. The Norwegians had to acquiesce to the formation of a union with Sweden in which they shared a king and had joint defence arrangements and foreign policies; all other matters were to be dealt with separately by the two countries.

Between 1814 and 1905, Norway had its own constitution, government and Parliament, made its own laws and budgets, established its own university, national bank and currency, and so on; in short, the country bore all the hallmarks of an independent state, except for its defence arrangements and foreign policy. Thus, in almost all practical matters, Norway was a separate and self-governing state from 1814.

NORWAY: GENERAL INFORMATION AND HISTORY

Land and people

Norway is the westernmost country on the Scandinavian peninsula, sharing borders with Sweden, Finland and, in the far northeast, Russia. These borders are identical to those that existed in 1814. The country is long and narrow, stretching 1,750km in a straight line from the southernmost to the northernmost point on the mainland, but the country also includes the archipelago of Svalbard (Spitsbergen), which boasts the northernmost settlement in the world. The country comprises 323,878km² (excluding Svalbard, which is the size of Denmark); it is rocky and mountainous, and only a small percentage of the land can be used for agriculture. Most of northern Norway is situated above the Arctic Circle.

Norway has five million inhabitants (as of 2012), approximately 0.6 million of whom live in the capital Oslo, with another 0.6 million residing in the region surrounding the capital. Its other largest cities are Bergen (with 260,000 inhabitants), Trondheim (174,000), Stavanger (126,000) and Kristiansand (83,000). The main city in northern Norway is Tromsø, which has a population of 68,000.

Norway has three long-standing minority languages: Sami and Finnish, both mainly spoken in the north, and Romani, spoken by some 500 Roma people who hold Norwegian passports. Sami is estimated to have 20,000–30,000 speakers, almost all of them bilingual. The Finnish-speaking minority, which is also entirely bilingual, is quite small today, perhaps numbering up to 2,000 speakers.

Starting in the late 1960s and early 1970s, Norway has received a substantial number of immigrants and refugees from non-Western countries. While these new Norwegian citizens have settled all over the country, most of them reside in and around Oslo. New Norwegian ethnolects have emerged which contain salient and easily identifiable prosodic features; these have been referred to as 'Kebab Norwegian' (cf. Østby 2005; Opsahl 2010) or, in job advertisements by the Norwegian

Broadcasting Corporation, as 'foreign dialects', a term which is to be interpreted to mean new dialects/ethnolects of Norwegian.

Brief overview of Norway's history and language

Norway came into being as a separate political entity around the year 900, when King Harald the Fairhaired united smaller kingdoms into one. The written documentation from this age is limited to inscriptions on rocks and other hard objects such as metal and bones. These inscriptions are written in the alphabet known as the Younger Futhark (runes).

Rune carving in Scandinavia dates as far back as the third century AD, and from these old texts it is clear that the language used in Norway in prehistoric times was a common Nordic/Scandinavian branch of North Germanic, which was found all over Scandinavia.

In the year 1030, Christianity became established in Norway, and in 1152 Norway was granted its own Roman Catholic archbishop. The Church introduced both the Latin alphabet and writing on parchment. The first documents written in (Old) Norwegian date from the middle of the twelfth century and reveal a language which differs from contemporary Swedish and Danish.

Politically speaking, the Norwegian kingdom became an important European power in the twelfth and thirteenth centuries. The realm consisted of Norway proper (including three areas that now belong to Sweden: Båhuslen, Jemtland and Herjedalen), Iceland, Greenland, the Faroe Islands, the Shetland Islands, the Orkneys, the Hebrides and the Isle of Man. Writing in Old Norwegian/Old Norse was used extensively throughout the kingdom, and continental European medieval literature was also translated into Norwegian during this period. (On the language of the period, cf. Seip [1931] 1971; Indrebø 1951; Haugen 1976, 1982.)

Until about 1300, Old Norwegian and Old Icelandic were quite similar. Iceland had been colonised by Norway around 900, and the cultural and political ties between Norway and Iceland were therefore quite strong. In the 1220s, the Icelandic writer and chieftain, Snorre Sturlason (1179–1241), wrote down the chronicles of the Norwegian kings up to the year 1179; this book proved to be of great importance to Norway during the nineteenth and twentieth centuries in its process of nation building.

Although the kingdom of Norway was a major power in the thir-teenth century, a period of decline occurred in the fourteenth century. The north European trade 'empire', the Hanseatic League, was very influential in the fourteenth and fifteenth centuries, with the city of Bergen serving as one of its main settlements outside Germany. The Norwegian, Danish and Swedish languages were heavily influenced by Low German, the language of the Hanseatic traders, over a period of several hundred years. During this time, the three languages changed from being predominantly synthetic to basically analytic in structure. In contrast, Icelandic preserved its synthetic structure, as the country had much less contact with the Hanseatic League (Haugen 1976: 313–20; Jahr 2001; Elmevik and Jahr 2012).

Starting in the 1380s, a series of dynastic unions between the three kingdoms of Norway, Sweden and Denmark resulted eventually in the union of Denmark-Norway from the fifteenth century onwards, during which Norway was increasingly treated as a Danish colony. The Old Norwegian (Old Norse) language of the Middle Ages disap-peared little by little, and written Danish prevailed throughout the Dano-Norwegian kingdom. In addition, Lutheranism was intro-duced into Denmark-Norway in 1537, thus putting an end to several centuries of Catholicism.

After the Dano-Norwegian union ended in 1814, and during the bilateral union of Sweden and Norway from 1814 to 1905, Norway gradually built up its national institutions and developed its political system, moving from a clear division of power between Parliament and the government to a parliamentary system, which was introduced in 1884 after a fierce political battle lasting several years. Since then, the government has always been directly responsible to Parliament, and thus has been forced to resign after losing an important vote.

What finally caused the Swedish-Norwegian union to collapse in 1905 was the demand by Norwegians to have their own foreign-based consulates. This was important to Norway, since the Norwegian economy was far more export oriented (mainly because of shipping) than the Swedish economy, and Norwegians therefore wanted their own representatives in place abroad. When this wish was repeat-edly denied by the King, the union was dissolved by the Norwegian Parliament on 7 June 1905. Although there was a danger of war breaking out between the two countries, subsequent negotiations eased the tense situation, and the parties were able to settle all their differences. The political insignificance of the nearly century-old union was demonstrated by the fact that almost no laws or regulations had to be changed or altered in either country as a result of the union's discontinuation.

During World War I, Norway successfully remained neutral and managed to stay out of the conflict. However, between 1940 and 1945, the country was occupied by Nazi Germany. Norway joined the NATO Alliance in 1949. In both 1972 and 1994, a majority of Norwegian citizens voted 'no' in a national referendum on joining the European Union; and in a poll conducted in August 2013, more than 70 per cent of the voters reported that they were against Norwegian membership of the EU (*Klassekampen*, 26 August 2013). Norway's historical background of political union, first with Denmark and then with Sweden, offers some explanation as to why the population has been reluctant to join this body.

Norway emerged in 1814 as one of the poorest countries in Europe. Today, however, it is one of the wealthiest. Most of its national revenue today derives from oil, various high-tech industries, and fisheries.

The country's population was one million in 1822 and two million in 1890. In 1942 it had grown to three million, rising to four million in 1975. And in the March 2012 census, the population of Norway was five million. In 2010, close to 80 per cent of the populace were members of the Lutheran Church.

LANGUAGE PLANNING

The study of language planning is a relatively new discipline within linguistics, originating as late as the 1960s. However, the activity itself has a much longer history, dating back to the establishment of language academies – in Florence (1582), France (1635), Spain (1713) and Sweden (1786). These language academies usually worked to preserve and defend the 'purity of language'. During the nineteenth century, the spread of literacy and growing demands for printed books, especially in Europe and America, created a greater perceived need for language standardisation. Political events led to the rise of new states, such as Norway (1814), Greece (1829), Finland (1917), Ireland (1921) and Israel (1948). These changes set in motion the establishment of new official languages in several countries, and in Israel saw the revival of Hebrew. The actual codifications of these languages were the result of work carried out by government committees, language academies or, in several cases – and as we will see in Norway – by individuals.

Language planning emerged as a separate branch of sociolinguistics, as just noted, in the 1960s, a time when interest rose in linguistic problems associated with multilingual situations, especially in new Third World countries, and there was a perceived need for a theory of language planning. This was also when Einar Haugen presented one of his many important works (1966a) on language planning in Norway, in which he outlined the first model constructed to describe language planning activities. By so doing, Einar Haugen contributed substantially to establishing this discipline.

Einar Haugen's 1966 model of language planning

Having studied extensively the linguistic development of modern Norway (that is, post-1814), Haugen (1966a and b) suggested a four-part model as a framework for language planning. After minor revisions (Haugen 1983), the model consisted of the following four elements:

1. *Selection of a norm*: the choice of which variety or varieties of language should be the object of the ensuing efforts.
2. *Codification* of the variety or varieties selected: choice of script, phonology and orthography, morphology and word-formation rules, syntax, and so on.
3. *Implementation*: the stage where the codified norm is introduced and disseminated throughout society.
4. *Elaboration*: the continuing effort to spread the norm and ensure it is capable of meeting different functional and other demands of society.

This model has proved most useful, and has been employed in many language-planning case studies of different countries and societies around the world.

An important distinction was introduced into this discipline by Heinz Kloss (1969): *language corpus planning* – that is, changes in spelling and morphology, coining of new terms, and adoption of new scripts – versus *language status planning* – that is, the relationship between languages and/or varieties of a language. This distinction has proved to be very useful, as it stresses two very important yet different aspects of language planning activities.

Haugen's model is perhaps more relevant for corpus planning than for status planning, and provides a useful tool for describing what language planners actually do. A full theoretical underpinning for language planning has not yet been developed. Such a theory of language planning would have to be capable of answering more than superficial questions concerning the driving forces behind specific language planning programmes. A more developed theory would strive to describe and explain all intentionally introduced linguistic changes, and aim at understanding and explaining successes and failures in language planning. It should be able to predict, or at least suggest, which language planning efforts are possible under which linguistic and cultural/sociopolitical circumstances.

However, in much of the literature, language planning is implicitly considered to be a purely technical process in which principles like 'economy', 'rationality', and 'efficiency' play a fundamental part. These aspects are, of course, highly important, but equally so is the fact that language planning is always conducted in a sociopolitical and hence ideological context. Any relevant theory must therefore take into consideration the fact that language planning is usually a response to strongly felt sociopolitical problems. Ideological perspectives as well as the political and social implications of different proposals have to be discussed, evaluated, understood and then incorporated into a theoretical framework in order for a more comprehensive theory of language planning to be developed.

Drawing on empirical data from the Norwegian case, this book aims at making specific contributions to such an endeavour.

Language corpus planning and language status planning

Language planning, then, refers to organised activities, private or official, which attempt to solve language problems within a given society, usually at the national level. Through language planning, attempts are made to direct, change or preserve the linguistic norm (*language corpus planning*) or the social status and communicative function of a given written or spoken language or variety of a language (*language status planning*). Language planning usually has a deliberate goal, follows a declared programme or a defined set of criteria and is carried out by officially appointed committees or bodies, by private organisations, or by prescriptive linguists often working on behalf of official authorities. The object is to establish norms, primarily written ones, which are validated through achieving high social status. Oral norms connected with these written standards may, but do not always, follow.

Norwegian language planning

Developments in the Norwegian language have been the object of considerable international interest. In 1932, a German scholar defended his Ph.D. thesis on the Norwegian language conflict (Meyen 1932). It was, however, through the publication of Einar Haugen's seminal monograph, *Language Conflict and Language Planning: The Case of Modern Norwegian* (1966a), that the Norwegian situation became a celebrated example of modern language planning and language conflict (cf. Gundersen 1967; Larson 1985; Jahr 1989b; Fishman 1997: 253–6; Bucken-Knapp 2003; Mesthrie et al. 2009: 393–7). However, neither Cooper (1989), Kaplan and Baldauf Jr (1997), nor the series *Language Planning and Policy in Europe* (in three volumes: Kaplan and Baldauf Jr 2005; Baldauf Jr and Kaplan 2006; Kaplan and Baldauf Jr 2008) offer any account of the special development of the Norwegian language.

Haugen opened his account by stating: 'Little by little a linguistic avalanche has been set in motion, an avalanche which is still [in 1966] sliding and which no one quite knows how to stop, even though many would be happy to do so' (Haugen 1966a: 1). Our task will now be to try and understand how the avalanche was set in motion, how and why it travelled in the direction it did, as well as how and why it slowed down and eventually came close to stopping after almost 200 years.

The only recognised Scandinavian languages in the first half of the nineteenth century were Danish, Swedish and Icelandic. From 1814 onwards, however, Norwegian entered into a phase of development as a language. This process will be divided into three main periods here, providing the structure for this book:

1. 1814–1917: the nationalist period, when national arguments dominated. The main goal during this period was to develop a national

linguistic standard. By 1917, the country had established two such standards.

2. 1917–66: the sociopolitical period, when social arguments were the driving force behind developments. The main political goal during this period was to reach a linguistic compromise between the two standards.

3. 1964–2002: the period of transition from a single-standard strategy of language planning (up until 1966) to a two-standard strategy. A Parliamentary decision in 2002 and language reforms in 2005 (for Bokmål) and 2012 (for Nynorsk) completed the process.

Most accounts of Norwegian language history from 1814 onwards have been very detail oriented, comprising an enormous amount of empirical data about various language reforms, the programmes and actions of the opposing parties in the language conflict, official documents discussing the linguistic situation, the treatment of the language issue in Parliament, in newspapers, and by local school boards, and so on. It is easy to get lost in all this data; many students therefore find studying this topic tiresome. While these historical accounts present details in a very systematic manner, they often fail to explain what all these data really tell us about the choices that were made and the actions that were taken. Few scholars have provided an analysis of the driving forces underlying the observable developments, or, even more importantly, a coherent explanatory model for the development of Norwegian through the nineteenth and twentieth centuries.

This book aims to offer such a model. Our focus will be on analysis and explanation more than on covering all aspects and details of language development, and the topics and data presented have been selected and structured in order to support this objective. The account will draw extensively on general results from the past forty to fifty years of research within the fields of language contact, sociolinguistics and the sociology of language. The book's major objective is to provide both an analysis of the development of Norwegian over almost 200 years, and an overall understanding of the motives, interests, organisations and political ideologies behind what appears to be the only well-documented attempt we have to change the sociolinguistic landscape of a European country through language planning.

PART I

THE NATIONALIST
PERIOD, 1814–1917

CHAPTER 2

Before the start of language planning: 1814–45

Political developments 1814–45

At the negotiations about a bilateral union with Sweden in the autumn of 1814, following the short war that August between the two countries, the Norwegians insisted on inserting a clause in their new Constitution stating that the business of the state should be conducted 'in Norwegian'. The phrase 'the Norwegian language' (*det norske Sprog*) is employed several times in the document (§§ 33, 47, 81).

Since nobody at the time had any clear view about what 'the Norwegian language' meant, other than denoting the Danish language which they shared with the Danes, it is obvious that this wording was in fact intended to convey the meaning 'not Swedish'. The laws and everything else pertaining to Norway were *not* to be written in Swedish, but rather in the written standard used in Norway. At the time this standard was Danish, as it had been for most of the time throughout the long union with Denmark.

However, while Denmark was no longer part of the political picture, Sweden definitely was, and it was obvious to everybody that the Crown Prince of Sweden, Carl Johan, intended to expand and strengthen the union as time went by. It became an important political goal for Norwegians to defend their Constitution, and Parliament refused to make any changes whatsoever to the text agreed upon by Norway and Sweden in November 1814.

The Constitution demarcated a three-way division of state power.

Parliament, which convened every third year, passed laws and determined the budget. The government was appointed by the King and was empowered to implement parliamentary legislation and run the country's national affairs; its cabinet ministers were recruited without exception from the upper-middle classes. Judicial power was vested in the courts, with the Supreme Court at the head.

Along with securing a sound economic basis for the new nation, Norway's relationship with Sweden – especially with the King, who from 1818 was Carl Johan – constituted the most important political issue in the years immediately following 1814. Norway's aim was to protect every inch of independence won in 1814 and stop any attempt to expand or strengthen the political union with Sweden.

The upper-middle classes consisted mostly of government officials (*embetsmenn*) who were university graduates holding important official positions, together with a tiny group of extremely wealthy merchants. However, it is also necessary to appreciate the fact that most of Norway's rural inhabitants were not tenant farmers or serfs, as was the case in Denmark and many other European countries. The Norwegian peasantry had always been free and owned their farms. However, land became more scarce as the population grew, and peasants who owned large farms started to hand over parcels of land in exchange for a specified number of days' work on these farms every year in payment. This arrangement gave rise to a group of peasants who were dependent on the bigger farms and their owners. This group of more dependent peasants were called *huusmænd* (modern Norwegian: *husmenn*).

In the 1814 Constitution, the right to vote was given to all officials, citizens of towns, and every man who owned his own plot of land, however small. In Norway this meant that almost all of the peasantry, and 40 per cent of the total male population over twenty-five years of age, were handed the right to vote, which provided the peasants with a tremendous amount of political influence once they had learnt to use it. In the years immediately after 1814, they usually voted for their parish priest at parliamentary elections, which were held every third year. However, from the 1830s, peasants became aware of their political opportunities and started voting for their own representatives, subsequently filling Parliament with Members of Parliament who saw it as their duty to work for the common interests of the peasant class.

In western Norway, most of the peasants owned small farms, while in the eastern half of the country, the farms were larger. In northern Norway, land-owning peasants often combined farming with fishing, as the small farms could not provide enough income for a family to live on, and fishing provided a necessary supplement to their income. This social difference between the various parts of the country would in the ensuing century play an important role in both politics in general and language policy in particular. The wealthier farmers in the eastern half of the country tended to side with the upper-middle classes in politics and, consequently, to a great extent also when it came to the language issue.

The Constitution, then, made it possible for peasants to obtain a majority in Parliament, since suffrage had been given to all landowners, whatever the size of their holdings. In 1833 this led to the first Parliament which had an absolute majority of peasant representatives. 'The Peasant Parliament' (*Bondestortinget*), as it was called, followed a careful and conservative economic policy, allowing only very limited government spending; it was also conservative in cultural matters and represented traditional peasant values.

One of the most important decisions during the 1830s and 1840s was taken by Parliament in 1838 with The Local Self-Governance Act (*Formandskabslovene*). This law stipulated that voters in every municipality, city and town were to elect a body of local representatives imbued with the authority to decide on matters concerning schools, care for the poor, road construction and other local affairs. These bodies were also to determine the level of local taxes to finance their various undertakings. This reform proved to be of tremendous importance in the following decades, as local representatives all over the country were introduced to political work, and could later be recruited to central political positions, for example Parliament. Many peasant members of Parliament in the second half of the nineteenth century received their initial political training while serving on their local municipal councils. The 1838 Act thus contributed substantially to the democratic development of Norwegian society during the nineteenth century.

Taking a longer perspective, the social difference between the government, which consisted entirely of members of the upper-middle classes, and Parliament, which had a majority from the peasant class, led to major conflicts of interest surfacing, something which became more and more obvious with every new parliamentary session. In the second half of the nineteenth century, this was also to have a tremendous impact on language policy.

The linguistic situation around 1814

Sociolinguistically speaking, the situation in 1814 was quite 'normal': the spoken language used among the upper-middle classes throughout the country was closely connected to the written standard, which was essentially Danish, and peasants' and fishermen's dialects were considered to be of low social status and were thus only used locally.

During the long union with Denmark, rural dialects within Norway were seen as, and also referred to as, Danish dialects, a view made possible by the close linguistic relationship between Danish and Norwegian. After 1814, Norwegian dialects had to be labelled differently, but it took a few decades before what they had to offer linguistically to the important nation-building process became apparent.

Written Danish had been firmly established as a language standard by the beginning of the nineteenth century (Jacobsen 2010). The first official royal decree about Danish orthography dates from 1739. For Denmark-Norway before 1814, the most important language directive singled out a specific book as the model for Danish orthography: Ove Malling's *Great and Good Actions by Danes, Norwegians and Holsteiners* (*Store og gode Handlinger af Danske, Norske og Holstenere*), published in 1777 (ibid.). This book served as a model for written Danish orthography in Norway in the nineteenth century, long after it was clearly outdated in Denmark itself. Interestingly, the Norwegians proved to be more conservative with regard to Danish orthography in the nineteenth century than the Danes themselves.

In the second half of the eighteenth century, and thirty-four years before the dissolution of the Dano-Norwegian union, a priest of Danish origin working in southern Norway, Jacob Nicolaj Wilse, wrote that the Danish spoken by the upper-middle classes in Christiania had the most pleasing pronunciation of all the spoken varieties of Danish; moreover, it was also the one closest to the written standard (Hyvik 2009: 121–123).

The reason for Wilse's judgement – which he did not mention – was that spoken Danish, in Denmark, had long before that time developed away from the pronunciation reflected in the orthography of the written standard, and these changes most often had no parallel in Norway. Instead, the spoken variety used by the Norwegian upper-middle classes reflected – because it was based on – the Danish written form, and thus was much closer to the written Danish standard (cf. Haraldsrud 2012):

Written Danish around 1800	Danish pronunciation	Upper-middle-class speech in Norway early nineteenth century	
Lærer	/læ:a/	/læ:rer/	'teacher'
Løøg	/lo:j/	/lø:g/	'onion'
Sag	/sæ:w/	/sa:g/	'saw, n.'
Kage	/kæ:e/	/ka:ge/	'cake'

While this upper-class oral variety was clearly non-Danish in terms of prosody, phonology and syntax, the word forms, morphology and vocabulary had been derived from the written Danish of the eighteenth century – in the first instance by Norwegians who did not have Danish as their native language and therefore used the written language as their model.

Following Trudgill (1986), this product of contact between Norwegian and Danish may be termed a *koiné* or *creoloid*. Creoloids are mixed languages and – like creoles – are mother-tongue languages, but unlike creoles they have no prior history as pidgins. Consider Afrikaans, which is a celebrated example of a creoloid. While it has descended over the centuries from the Dutch of the original Boers of South Africa, Afrikaans was greatly influenced, not least in terms of structural simplification, by contact with other languages in the region, while never totally losing contact with Dutch. Likewise, the Dano-Norwegian variety of the upper-middle classes had no history as a pidgin in 1814. On the contrary, it became the mother tongue of its speakers and never went through a period of the functional reduction which is characteristic of a pidgin. Indeed, it was totally intelligible to speakers of Danish, as well as to speakers of Norwegian dialects, though it exhibited instances of grammatical simplification and levelling, as well as admixture.

For example, while all local dialects in Norway – except for the city of Bergen – had a three-gender system (masculine, feminine and neuter), in the Dano-Norwegian creoloid this was simplified to two genders, following the Danish written standard, which also has only two genders (common and neuter). In the past tense of the largest group of weak verbs, the creoloid had developed its own ending -*et*, diverging both from written Danish (-*ede*) and from Norwegian dialects, most of which had -*a*. However, it had adopted the Norwegian dialect system of employing the same ending for both the past tense and perfect participle, which is simplified compared to the Danish pattern of having the past tense in -*ede* and the perfect participle in -*et*. The Dano-Norwegian creoloid thus was grammatically simplified with respect to written Danish and had adopted the system of the Norwegian dialects. Its lexicon and word forms were drawn mainly from written Danish, while the phonology and syntax were basically non-Danish, and the morphology was mixed. Its prosody had a closer relationship to western Swedish prosody (cf. Riad 2006).

By the nineteenth century, members of the upper and educated classes spoke this creoloid as their first and only native linguistic variety. As the speech of the upper-middle classes, and in spite of being an obvious result of language contact, this variety has enjoyed the highest social status of all spoken varieties in Norway. Throughout the nineteenth century, it was given various names and was characterised in different ways; since the late 1890s it has often been referred to as spoken *Riksmål*.

The field of linguistics in the nineteenth century was dominated by the comparative historical method and, later, the Neogrammarian approach. These theories played pivotal roles in the debate concerning the language question after 1814, thus defining in many ways the direction and arguments of the nineteenth-century language debate. However, they were incapable of providing an adequate framework for the analysis and description of what – from the viewpoint of modern language contact theory – was the type of unique result of language contact found among the speech of the Norwegian upper-middle classes. The fact that entirely new varieties could develop out of language contact was in principle beyond the conceptual apparatus of these theories, which were not able to handle any consequences of language contact apart from borrowing.

Why did language create a problem in Norway after 1814?

The sociolinguistic situation in Norway at the time of its independence in 1814 resembles what we find in many Western societies today: there is a spoken, high-status variety (the Dano-Norwegian creoloid) used by the upper-middle classes throughout the country, and low-status vernacular dialects used by the country's peasants and fishermen. This situation could easily have continued without being seriously questioned – had it not been for three important circumstances:

1. the rise of national romanticism as an influential philosophical movement of the period;
2. the fact that Norway's written standard was Danish, and as such – after 1814 – belonged to a foreign country; and
3. the fact that the prestigious spoken variety of the upper-middle classes was the result of language contact during the Dano-Norwegian union.

This new, unique spoken Scandinavian variety would turn out to be the surprise element in the language conflicts which grew in intensity over the decades after 1814 and which did not finally die down until the very end of the twentieth century.

Had the historic events of 1814 happened about a century earlier, there might never have been any conflict over the Norwegian language. Like the United States, which carried on using English after their War of Independence of 1775–83, Norway perhaps would have continued to use written Danish, and have considered the sharing of a common language over a larger geographical area as advantageous.

However, National Romantic ideology, which was current in Germany around 1800, had a major cultural influence on Norway (cf. Falnes 1933). An essential and – for the new nation – existential question arose. Language, according to this philosophic movement, is the primary symbol of a separate and independent nation. National Romanticism held that a nation expresses itself, and its unique and distinctive qualities, through its own language.

So what was the distinctive language of Norway which expressed the special qualities of what Norwegians now claimed to be a separate nation? And what differentiated it from the language of the Danes and the Swedes, which were nonetheless intelligible to Norwegians and thus very closely linked linguistically? There were historical and political reasons behind Danish and Swedish being considered different languages at that time. However, today, from a purely linguistic point of view, Swedish, Danish and Norwegian can equally well be considered to be a single Scandinavian language with three main standardised varieties – or four, since Norwegian today comes in two standards.

The shared written language in the Dano-Norwegian union up to 1814 was often referred to as 'The Common Language' (*Fællessproget*), and yet once Norway was separated politically from Denmark, language became a contentious cultural and political issue over the course of a few decades. The question of a Norwegian language surfaced and needed to be addressed. How could, or should, the new nation develop a language standard of its own, with national characteristics which made it worthy of the name 'Norwegian'?

It is commonly argued that Norwegians became better writers of Danish after the union was dissolved in 1814 than they had ever been before. An improved educational system is often given as the reason for this development. Upon closer inspection, however, it turns out that literacy was not that widespread among the general population in the decades immediately following independence from Denmark. It was not until the close of the nineteenth century that the literacy rate rose to a high level (Vannebo 1984). Knud Knudsen and Ivar Aasen, the two major nineteenth-century language planners who we will meet in Chapter 3, were both particularly concerned about literacy and wanted to make it easier for common people to learn to read and use the written standard.

It is nevertheless interesting to take as our starting point the claim that 'Norwegians' became better at writing Danish soon after 1814, since it is found in nearly all Norwegian language history textbooks. The statement begs the following question: who were these 'Norwegians'? Or rather: who in Norway constituted the Norwegian nation? We will see in the next chapter that the answer to this question had far-reaching consequences for how one evaluated the linguistic situation in Norway in the nineteenth century.

Most Norwegians consider their country to be ancient, dating at least from around 900 when Harald the Fairhaired united the country under one king. This view has been so ingrained in most Norwegians since their school days that they rarely venture to question it. But occasionally someone does point out that Norway is in fact a rather young European nation – it will celebrate only its bicentenary in 2014. The question of how old Norway is might appear somewhat strange in the present context. However, it is an important factor in understanding the language debate and language developments during the nineteenth century, as it is precisely through formulating questions about the age of the country that one may gain insights into why there was a 'language issue' in Norway in the first place – and why it took the form and direction it did (Jahr 1986).

The journal *Saga* (1816)

The first public discussions about language in the new nation took place as early as 1816. These soon became quite intense, due to Parliament's constant fear that Sweden would attempt to expand and strengthen the union during its early years.

Jacob Aall (1773–1844), an iron-mill owner, and Johan Storm Munch (1778–1832), a clergyman and later a bishop, together launched a new journal in 1816 called *Saga*, which included a limited number of short translations – in the accepted Danish written standard – of old Icelandic sagas. Interestingly, these translations happened to use some Swedish words or word forms, for example, *øde* 'destiny' (Danish: *skjæbne*); *torpare* 'tenant farmer' (Danish: *huusmand*); and *drotning* 'queen' (Danish: *dronning*). A Member of Parliament fiercely attacked their use of these Swedish words, seeing this as a treacherous attempt at merging the languages, and he predicted – in a brief booklet published the following year – that this should make people fear a subsequent political amalgamation of Sweden and Norway (Hyvik 2002).

Although the ensuing discussion was intense and passionate for a while, it soon became quite clear that the Swedes had no intention whatsoever of striving for a linguistic merger. Thus, the first language conflict in the new nation faded away after a relatively short time (Seip 1913; Hyvik 2009: 194–203).

An easy solution that could have worked

As we saw above, the Constitution of November 1814 referred to 'the Norwegian language'. Quite soon after that, it became more or less official policy to call the written standard inherited from the Dano-Norwegian union 'Norwegian' when used in Norway.

The Christiania University Board issued a statement in 1815 that argued for and defended this usage (Indrebø 1951: 358; Hoel 1996: 48), and the headmaster of the capital's cathedral school published the first brief history of the Norwegian language in 1816, in which he also defended the use of the term 'Norwegian' for the written standard (Burgun 1919: 69f.).

This usage continued through the 1820s along with the more neutral term 'mother tongue', for example in the titles of school text-books and grammar books. In 1828, a law professor at the university wrote four newspaper articles in which he defended using 'Norwegian' for the common written standard found in Denmark and Norway, when applied to Norway (Hoel 1996: 49, 382). His main argument, similar to that issued by the university board, was that during the centuries-long Dano-Norwegian union, authors from Norway had contributed substantially to the development of the Danish written standard; therefore, his reasoning went, Norway had the same claim to the common standard, and it could rightfully be called 'Norwegian' when used in Norway, just as it was called 'Danish' when used in Denmark.

This argument was rejected by Danish linguists and was to a certain extent ridiculed in Denmark. Nevertheless, the idea achieved a rather strong level of official support in Norway. This was the case until 1832, when a twenty-two-year-old law and history student, Peter Andreas Munch, published an article in which he totally rejected the idea that the written standard could be called anything other than Danish (Munch 1832; Hyvik 2012).

Even though 'Norwegian' continued to be used for the common written standard in Denmark and Norway into the 1830s, it was increasingly replaced with phrases such as 'the written language', 'the mother tongue', 'the common language', 'the usual book language'.

The fact that a twenty-two-year-old university student could effectively repudiate all the former statements and arguments put forward for the use of the term 'Norwegian', and do so through the publication of just a single article (divided into two parts and published in two separate issues of the journal *Vidar*), testifies to the enormous intellectual authority that P. A. Munch had already achieved at a very young age. Years later, when he was a professor, Munch wrote favourably about Ivar Aasen's works and negatively about Knud Knudsen's language programme (as we will see in Chapter 3), and this had a strong impact on how the intelligentsia received and viewed both Aasen and Knudsen in the second half of the nineteenth century.

Figure 2.1   Henrik Wergeland (1808–45), made from a lost daguerreotype picture. (Source: I. W. Tegner & Kittendorffs lith. Inst./National Library of Norway.)

Had the easy solution of calling the common written standard 'Norwegian' won general acceptance in both Norway and Denmark at this time, Norway might not have experienced one hundred and fifty years of language planning and linguistic conflict. Munch's 1832 article is therefore perhaps the most important publication about the language prior to the works of Aasen and Knudsen.

However, the primary target of Munch's article was not the use of 'Norwegian' as the name for the written standard. His main concerns were the ideas about language and the linguistic practice of the young poet Henrik Wergeland (1808–45).

Henrik Wergeland's idea about developing a Norwegian language

In the 1830s, Henrik Wergeland, who is regarded in Norway as the foremost national bard, argued strongly for a reform of the written standard in order to move it in what he considered to be a more 'Norwegian' direction. He adhered to this principle in his own writings, using distinctively Norwegian words when he felt the need for them, as well as creating entirely new words based on Norwegian roots.

In doing this, Wergeland was following the previously expressed thoughts of Jacob Aall and others (cf. Hyvik 2009: 202). In a speech given in 1811 to celebrate the Dano-Norwegian king establishing the first university in Norway, Aall presented his ideas about how the university, which was to open in 1813, could aid Norway's linguistic development. He predicted that the language of Norway – and by this he meant the written language – would evolve into a different variety from the Danish standard used at the time. Aall was one of the first to suggest that linguistic material from Norwegian dialects might be incorporated into the Danish written standard, and that through this Danish would be modified into a more suitable standard for use in Norway. He also foresaw a positive qualitative change coming from this since, as he put it, Danish 'culture' would merge with Norwegian 'nature' and 'freshness'. The journal *Saga* that he and J. S. Munch started in 1816 was a first attempt to substantiate this idea, and thus it was unfortunate that their use of a few Swedish words in the translations from Old Norse was what caught the public's attention.

The romantic poet Henrik Wergeland's 'Norwegianisation' of the written standard mainly involved using lexical items that were not found in Danish, most of them pertaining to nature and daily life in Norway. Wergeland – who was considered by certain people to be daring and careless – utilised words, idioms and forms taken from spoken Norwegian in his writing (Seip 1914). He argued that this was necessary for national, stylistic and democratic reasons (Wergeland 1835 [written in 1832]). Moreover, Wergeland predicted that before 'the century has run its course' (*før Aarhundrede nedrødmer*), the country would create 'an independent written language'. The reaction to Wergeland's usages triggered a broad public debate in the 1830s, a discussion that later proved to be the point of departure for the work of both Ivar Aasen and Knud Knudsen.

Asbjørnsen and Moe's collections of fairytales from the 1840s

In the 1840s, Peter Christen Asbjørnsen (1812–55), a zoologist and writer (Popp 1977), and Jørgen Moe (1813–82), a priest and later a bishop, continued Wergeland's task of Norwegianisation in several of their fairytale collections, which paralleled the Grimm brothers' collections of German stories. Asbjørnsen and Moe demonstrated that it was possible to employ what has been described as a unique 'Norwegian style and melody' in the written standard. This somewhat vague phrase describes writing which reflects oral style more than was usual in contemporary written texts, which quite often were heavily influenced by German and Latin stylistic patterns. What Asbjørnsen and Moe brought to the written standard was a more vernacular, straightforward type of syntax and style, modelled on informal daily speech, found in both popular dialects and upper-middle-class speech.

The first attempt at a sociolinguistic description – Jonas Anton Hielm's 1832 article

The first individual who attempted to provide a sociolinguistic description of Norway was a lawyer, Jonas Anton Hielm (1782–1848). In his introduction to an article published in May 1832 about Norwegian folk music, he divided the language into three main 'dialects' (Hielm 1832).

As he saw it, one dialect was found in the mountain areas; he wrote that it was close to Old Norwegian/Norse, especially in the most remote areas furthest away from the cities. A different dialect was spoken in the cities and towns, which Hielm speculated could be called a dialect of Danish, although it was modified by both the Norwegian spoken outside towns and the written standard. The third dialect he termed 'a so-called written language', similar to that found in Denmark, although modified with Norwegian words by some speakers.

This description is not as primitive as it might first appear, and we will later discover that the main sociolinguistic divide in Norwegian is clearly found between the spoken variety of the middle to upper classes on the one hand, and all the popular non-elite/folk dialects on the other. This seems to be what Hielm was trying to describe as the difference between his dialect of the mountain areas (= all the popular, non-elite dialects), as opposed to that of the cities and towns (= middle- to upper-class speech, the Dano-Norwegian creoloid). This latter variety is what Knud Knudsen later called 'educated colloquial speech' (*den dannede Dagligtale*) and also 'the nationwide Norwegian pronunciation' (*den landsgyldige norske Udtale*) (Knudsen 1876).

Hielm's third 'dialect' must be what at the time was often referred to as the 'oral language used in lectures and speeches'. This was a very formal variety used, for instance, when reading aloud from a manuscript, and therefore was as closely linked to the written standard as possible. It was basically a spelling pronunciation of the Danish written standard; however, as Hielm states, it was randomly modified with individual Norwegian words to express items or concepts typical of Norwegian nature or everyday life that did not occur in Danish. This variety was sometimes called by the derogatory name 'sexton or schoolteacher Danish' (*klokkerdansk*).

Hielm supported Wergeland's idea about developing a written standard based on the 'dialect' of the cities and towns, which in his view was the best suited for implementing such a process.

Opposition to Wergeland's ideas and practice

Wergeland's ideas soon met with strong opposition, the most serious coming from P. A. Munch in the 1832 article mentioned above entitled 'Norwegian language reform' (*Norsk Sprogreformation*). In this article, Munch completely rejected the notion that it would be possible to alter written Danish so that it was more Norwegian without creating a state of complete linguistic chaos. Munch felt that written Danish in Norway should be kept as it was, and he saw it as advantageous for Norway to maintain its cultural ties with Denmark. If anything was to be done, he wrote, the enthusiastic language reformers should inform the public about Old Norse, as this would stimulate linguistic awareness among the general public. He also wrote that selecting one of the more archaic rural dialects, then comparing it with and modifying it in the direction of Old Norse, would provide a better solution to the problem than the hotchpotch of written Danish and spoken

Norwegian suggested by Wergeland and his followers. There is no reason, though, to believe that Munch truly thought his suggestion of modifying an archaic dialect with Old Norse would ever be carried out and offered as a national written standard for Norwegian.

However, it is interesting to note that the young Ivar Aasen read Munch's article. We cannot know for sure whether reading this particular paper was what triggered Aasen's lifelong work of creating a standard Norwegian language. In 1836, at the age of twenty-two, Aasen recorded his thoughts about his country's language situation, making a clear reference to Munch when writing that no single dialect should form the basis for the written standard, which should instead be based on all the popular dialects (Aasen [1836] 1909). From this, it seems fair to claim that Munch's 1832 article, directed mainly against Wergeland's own language usage and programme for language reform, also helped Aasen to formulate his more revolutionary programme for creating a totally new Norwegian standard which was to be a synthesis of all the Norwegian rural dialects.

The *status quo* position

One major position taken on the language question has received very little attention in literature and research on Norway's language development in the nineteenth century: the *status quo*. Full attention has been given to those individuals who suggested that something *had* to happen linguistically in the newly established state. Since something did indeed happen, the opinion of the vast majority of people at the time – who were either totally uninterested in language matters or who were in favour of sharing a common written standard with Denmark – has clearly been neglected in the literature (Bleken 1966).

P. A. Munch obviously sided with the majority, as expressed in his influential 1832 article. Later, however, his more or less passing thought from the same article that it would be far better to select an archaic peasant dialect and adapt it in the direction of Old Norse than implement what he regarded as Wergeland's chaotic linguistic programme has claimed most of the attention. Munch's primary concern was to keep the Danish standard as it was, and he felt it would be advantageous for Norway to retain this linguistic legacy from the time of the Dano-Norwegian union. This view has been greatly under-represented in previous accounts of Norwegian language development, but Achille Burgun deals with this *status quo* position in his account of the various positions taken in the 1850s (Burgun 1921: 33ff.).

Terminological notes concerning the written standards and upper-middle-class speech

The current names of the two Norwegian written standards, *Bokmål* and *Nynorsk*, became official terms in 1929 when Parliament passed legislation on the matter. Before this time, the corresponding terms were *Riksmål* and *Landsmål* (the letter '*å*', pronounced [ɔ:], was introduced as optional for '*aa*' in 1917, and was compulsory from 1938 onwards).

'Landsmaal' was the term Ivar Aasen chose for the standard he created (of which, more in Chapter 3), and he suggested the usage of this name from 1853 onwards. From Aasen's point of view, it meant the 'language of the country or realm' (*maalet i landet*). However, since Aasen drew only on rural dialects and did not consider the language of cities and towns during his fieldwork, to many people Landsmaal simply meant the 'rural language of the countryside' (*maalet paa landet*). Landsmaal supporters found this to be an irritating misconception, and quite early in the twentieth century they started looking for a more suitable name for their standard in order to get away from this rural image. (Their first suggestion – to call Landsmaal 'Norwegian' and Riksmaal 'Danish' – was, understandably enough, immediately rejected.)

The term 'Riksmaal' was made popular by the author Bjørnstjerne Bjørnson (1832–1910), who used it (*rigsmaal*) in a speech given in late November 1899 to refer to the Dano-Norwegian written standard, after which the term spread rapidly. During the second half of the nineteenth century, the usual name for this variety had been 'the common book language' (*det almindelige bogsprog*), or just 'the written language' (*skriftsproget*). However, Knud Knudsen and others used the term 'Dano-Norwegian' (*dansk-norsk*).

In the chronological account that follows, the terms that are closest to those actually used at the time will be employed. Therefore, we will use 'Danish' for the period from 1814 until 1862, the year of the first Norwegian reform of the Danish standard as it was written in Norway; after 1862, we will call it 'Dano-Norwegian' to distinguish it from the Danish used in Denmark. Between 1899 and 1929 we will use the term 'Riksmaal' (from 1917 spelt 'Riksmål') – 'language of the realm'; and after 1929 it becomes 'Bokmål'. For Aasen's standard, we will use the term 'Landsmaal' for the period up to 1929 (from 1917 spelt 'Landsmål'), and from then on it will be called 'Nynorsk'.

The spoken variety of the elite, or upper-middle classes, has been given a number of names over the years. When dealing with nineteenth-century developments, we will refer to this variety as the 'Dano-Norwegian creoloid' and 'upper-middle-class speech'. The first term points to the variety's origin: language contact during the Dano-Norwegian union. The term 'creoloid', as noted above, has been taken from Trudgill (1986). If one wants to emphasise the fact that Danish and Norwegian are closely related in a linguistic sense, and are usually mutually intelligible – albeit often with some difficulty – then we are dealing not with language contact but rather with dialect contact which, according to Trudgill (ibid.), may result in a variety which he calls a 'koiné'. Nevertheless, we choose to treat Danish and Norwegian as they are dealt with in almost every textbook and linguistic encyclopaedia – as separate languages. Bear in mind, however, that they are defined as two languages for the most part because of historical and political developments, and hardly at all for linguistic reasons.

The supporters of Riksmål did not accept the name Bokmål when it was first introduced in 1929. They also completely rejected the later corpus-planning language reforms of 1938 and looked for ways to maintain their variety as a reflection of upper-middle-class speech, which during the twentieth century was most often referred to as 'educated speech' (*dannet tale*) or 'spoken Riksmål' (*talt riksmål*). In our account of the twentieth century, we will use 'spoken Riksmål' alongside 'upper-middle-class speech', since this makes it easier to explain and understand the close relationship between this oral variety and a privately standardised written norm, also called 'Riksmål', which emerged in the early 1950s as a competitor to official Bokmål (see Chapter 7).

After World War II, the organised opposition to the official language planning policy started its own private programme of standardising Riksmål in order to move it away from the official Bokmål standard and keep it as close as possible to spoken Riksmål. This action created a confusing and – especially for teachers and schoolchildren – problematic rift between the official Bokmål norm, which was standardised by the authorities, and the private Riksmål norm, which was standardised outside official language planning programmes.

As this book unfolds, these terms, and others, will need additional explanation, since in fact the situation became more complicated with each language reform during the twentieth century, as the terms occasionally changed their meaning (cf. also the list of terms, pp. 193–7).

CHAPTER 3

A language based on upper-middle-class speech or peasant dialects? The programmes proposed by Knud Knudsen and Ivar Aasen

KNUD KNUDSEN (1812–95): 'NORWAY BEGAN IN 1814'

Biography: work beyond language planning

Knud Knudsen was the man who in theory and practice came to represent the view that the Norwegian language question should be resolved by developing the ideas of Jacob Aall, and even more so those of Henrik Wergeland. Knudsen argued in favour of this solution his entire life.

He was born 1812 in Holt, a parish in the vicinity of Tvedestrand, a small coastal town located in the southernmost region of the country, close to where Aall owned a large iron mill. Aall later supported Knudsen for several years when he was studying philology at university.

Knudsen's father was a local schoolteacher. Knud helped his father at school from the early age of nine years. He graduated from high school in 1832 and went on to study at university in the capital, where he earned a degree in philology in 1840, and then started his career as a teacher. In 1852 he was promoted to Headmaster at the Cathedral School in Christiania, a position he held until his retirement in 1880. Knudsen died in 1895 at the age of eighty-three (Johnsen 2006).

Figure 3.1　Knud Knudsen (1812–95), photo. (Source: unknown.)

Knudsen remained a bachelor all his life, dedicating himself first and foremost to developing a language standard as well as to addressing various pedagogical issues of the period. As a student in the 1830s, he was already involved in an attempt to reduce the dominance of classical Greek and Latin in higher education (Dahl 1962). For instance, the abolition of the Latin translation exam in high schools in 1857 was regarded as one of Knudsen's victories. The introduction of science as an elective subject alongside Latin in high schools was also a change for which Knudsen had argued (Johnsen 2006).

Nevertheless, Knudsen's main interest and most important contribution was the language programme he proposed. His 1856 grammar text, *Handbook of Dano-Norwegian Grammar* (*Haandbog i dansk-norsk Sproglære*), proved that he was quite an innovative and independent grammarian (cf. Bleken 1956). In numerous articles, books and booklets published throughout his life, Knudsen passionately promoted and argued for his views and his proposed language standard, calling his programme 'the Dano-Norwegian language endeavour' (*det dansk-norske sprogstrev*); moreover, it became his lifelong pursuit to see this programme implemented.

While Knudsen lived to see some small yet significant aspects of his proposal accepted by the authorities (as we will see below), the real breakthrough for his programme came with the language reforms of 1907 and 1917 – well after his death.

Knudsen's language programme

In 1845, Knudsen published his first major article on the language problem, entitled 'On the sounds, phonetic symbols and orthography of the Norwegian language' (*Om Lydene, Lydtegnene og Retskrivningen i det norske Sprog*). He followed this up in 1850 with his article 'On Norwegianness in our speech and writing' (*Om Norskhed i vor Tale og Skrift*). These two publications were of great significance, since they presented Knudsen's ideas about the development of a national written standard.

His proposals implied a step-by-step Norwegianisation process which would gradually transform the written language to reflect 'the common pronunciation of words from the mouths of the educated' (*den almindeligste udtale af ordene i de dannedes mund*). It was only at a much later stage (1876) that Knudsen came up with the less precise expression 'the nationwide Norwegian pronunciation' (*den landsgyldige norske uttale*). The social basis of this spoken variety – which in 1845 was overtly expressed in the phrase 'the educated' – is concealed in the later term.

Knudsen's initial 1845 publication was influenced by the Danish linguist, Rasmus Rask (1787–1832), who had suggested reforming the Danish spelling system based on the principle that each sound should be represented by one letter only, and each letter should represent only one sound. The main objective was for spelling to agree more closely with current pronunciation, rather than reflecting etymology and tradition. Rask's principles were referred to as 'orthophony', especially in Norway, where they proved to be more influential than in Denmark itself.

Knudsen's reasons for supporting a more orthophonic spelling system were both pedagogical and democratic in nature; he stated that adoption of this principle would make it much easier for the general public to learn to read and write. However, the consequence of doing this would be quite different in Norway and Denmark, since the pronunciation of the language was so different in the two countries. This is clearly manifested in Knudsen's early publications (1845, 1850), in which he argued that the Dano-Norwegian creoloid, or upper-middle-class speech (in Knudsen's words, 'the pronunciation in the mouth of the educated'), was the spoken variety in Norway on which spelling reforms of the Danish standard should be based in order to develop a specifically Norwegian standard. The Norwegianisation of written Danish would thus take place over time, and the resulting standard would reflect upper-middle-class speech as closely as possible.

The majority of the members of the upper-middle classes were government officials and civil servants, who were scattered all over the country and whose idiom was thus heard throughout all regions. All members of government and all of the country's most prominent politicians came from this social group, and it was primarily their policies, efforts and contributions which had helped secure the country's independence and draw up its constitution.

Knudsen explained the rationale behind his choice for a norm as follows (1850: 214, author's translation):

The language of the population lacks uniformity, as the intercourse between the populations of different regions and country districts is far too infrequent to enable any linguistic differences to be evened out. On the other hand, the educated class does not belong in any particular region or landscape, but moves about and intermingles . . . This educated class is also more numerous than the users of any of our regional dialects, and it also possesses the highest levels of education and intellectual capacity, so it is not reasonable that it should bow to the general populace and teach itself or its children to speak their language, whom it in other respects governs and dominates intellectually.

Knudsen thus advocated a process that would transform written Danish into a Norwegian national standard which would reflect upper-middle-class speech as closely as possible. He considered this to be an obvious solution, the product of reason and of the evolutionary development of a written standard that had enough national characteristics to be worthy of the name 'Norwegian'.

One salient Norwegian feature he specifically focused on was the use of /p, t, k/ for Danish /b, d, g/ after long vowels, for example Dan. *tab* > *tap* ('loss'), Dan. *mad* > *mat* ('food'), Dan. *tag* > *tak* ('roof'). He also wanted to introduce shorter Norwegian-style forms of some frequently used verbs, for example *ha* < Dan. *have* ('have'), *la* < Dan. *lade* ('let'), *si* < Dan. *sige* ('say'), *ta* < Dan. *tage* ('take'), as well as for the kinship terms *bror* < Dan. *broder* ('brother'), *far* < Dan. *fader* ('father') and *mor* < Dan. *moder* ('mother').

Knudsen was very unhappy about the fact that, after independence, the upper-middle classes continued to use Danish linguistic models, specifically from the capital city Copenhagen. Throughout the 1830s, 1840s and 1850s, upper-middle-class speech showed a tendency to follow the latest Danish pronunciation trends. The reason for this was the predominant view among the elite that cultural ideals had traditionally come from the Danish capital, and language was seen as a natural part of the culture and refinement desired by the Norwegian bourgeoisie.

For example, with a few exceptions, Danish actors predominated in the theatres of the Norwegian capital. Moreover, the language of the stage was considered by many to represent 'correct' usage. This high level of public esteem for Danish pronunciation worried Knudsen a great deal, and as an advisor to a theatre in Christiania in the 1850s, he fought against what he considered to be characteristic Danish pronunciation on-stage (Burgun 1921: 15–20; Berg 1977). He espe-cially disliked the use of non-palatalised /k/ and /g/ before non-low vowels and diphthongs: words such as *kiste* ('chest'), *kære* ('dear'), *keiser* ('emperor'), *gift* ('poison') and *gyse* ('shiver') were pronounced with a /k/ or /g/ in Danish, but Knudsen promoted the Norwegian palatal pronunciation of these consonants, /ç/ and /j/, in such con-texts. He supported a protest in 1856 by Bjørnstjerne Bjørnson at a theatre in Christiania against the hiring of yet another Danish actor.

Even though Knudsen concentrated his efforts mainly on pronunciation in the theatre, his work to stop the Danicisation of upper-middle-class Norwegian speech also proved quite successful: by the 1880s there seems to have been no interest anymore among these speak-ers in bringing their variety more closely in line with spoken Danish. Knudsen's persistent arguments for choosing upper-middle-class speech as the basis for developing a Norwegian written standard had finally started to win broader support. However, this was also due to the political success of Ivar Aasen's proposed Landsmaal standard, which had truly started to frighten the upper-middle classes in the 1880s.

One reason it took so long for Knudsen's ideas to win support among members of the intelligentsia was Professor P. A. Munch's total rejection of Kundsen's endeavours as early as the 1850s and his simultaneous praise for Aasen's substantial contributions (that is, Aasen 1848 and 1850). While Munch described Aasen as a great lin-guist and scholar (Knudsen 1923: 64ff., 76ff.), he dismissed Knudsen as a 'linguistic bourbon' (ibid.: 100f.). Knudsen later wrote that Munch had wrapped him and his programme in thick fog from which he struggled for years to emerge (Johnsen 2006: 194).

However, in the second half of the 1880s, with the political pro-gress and success of Landsmaal (cf. p. 63 below), people could see that a linguistic revolution was coming, and this obviously upset the upper-middle classes and the intelligentsia considerably. Although this danger still loomed far off on the horizon, Knudsen's line of argument seemed at the time to provide quite a different and more acceptable route for the Norwegian elite to follow.

Reform of the written standard in 1862

The first official reform of the written standard was completed in 1862; from that year onwards, Danish in Denmark and Danish in

Norway were written somewhat differently from one another. The changes were limited to orthography and were a clear result of applying orthophonic principles. The person behind these reforms was Knudsen, who suggested the changes to the Ministry of Church and Education in 1860.

These reforms did away with certain consonants and combinations in the written standard: *ph* became *f*, while *ch*, *c* and *q* were replaced with *k*. Thus, the spelling of the capital Christiania (named after the Dano-Norwegian King Christian IV, who ruled from 1588 to 1648) changed to Kristiania (its name subsequently became Oslo in 1925). Certain vowels also underwent orthographic reform. The use of a double vowel to indicate length was eliminated, for example *huus* > *hus* ('house'), *iis* > *is* ('ice'). In monosyllables, a final long /i/ had been denoted by following it immediately with an *e*; this *e* was now discarded, as in *lie* > *li* ('hillside, mountainside').

So from 1862 onwards, we can distinguish between the Danish standard used in Denmark and the Danish standard used in Norway (called Dano-Norwegian here, which became Riksmaal/Riksmål in the twentieth century and finally Bokmål from 1929 onwards). The 1862 reforms took an important first step in Knudsen's mission to have the written standard in Norway considered as an entity in its own right, without reference to written Danish as used in Denmark. These changes could equally well have been undertaken in Denmark, too. The fact that they were only carried out in Norway proved that the Norwegians considered that the written standard used in Norway was, so to speak, Norwegian property, and could be managed according to Norwegian needs, plans and wishes, with no regard for how it was used in Denmark.

The next step in developing a Norwegian standard would be to implement changes that were not confined to orthography but which also involved phonology and morphology, again based exclusively on upper-middle-class speech.

Bjørnstjerne Bjørnson and Henrik Ibsen

Two major authors need to be mentioned as important figures behind the developments suggested by Knudsen: the already mentioned Bjørnstjerne Bjørnson (1832–1910) and Henrik Ibsen (1828–1906). Bjørnson was awarded the Nobel Prize for Literature in 1903, and

Ibsen was the world-famous playwright. Both contributed sub-stantially to the acceptance of Knudsen's programme by writing not in pure Danish but increasingly in a distinct Dano-Norwegian standard, whose style and syntax was based on what Knudsen called the 'educated colloquial speech' (*den dannede dagligtale*) of the upper-middle classes. This was especially salient in Bjørnson's early stories published in the 1850s (Seip 1916a), as well as in Ibsen's plays from the 1880s and onwards, where he utilised this variety of Norwegian speech in his dialogues (Knudsen 1967).

'Norwegianisation by degrees – evolution, not revolution!'

The programme for the development of a written standard put forward by Knudsen was motivated more by Knudsen the teacher and educator than by his nationalist persona. Indeed, Knudsen was not particularly preoccupied with the question of 'Danish' or 'Norwegian'. Rather, he felt it was important to create a written stand-ard in Norway that would meet the needs of as many of its language users as possible, in order to make it easier for the entire population to become literate. Knudsen therefore believed that the speech of the upper-middle classes was the only candidate variety from which to Norwegianise the written Danish standard – for use in Norway by Norwegians for Norwegians (Knudsen 1862, 1867, 1887).

Knudsen's approach defined Norway as a young nation which was 'born' in 1814. He was less concerned with retaining a linguistic con-nection back through the centuries to Old Norse and the Viking Age. He was much more interested in achieving practical results, that is easier access to reading and writing, than in national romantic ideas.

Knudsen often called the standard he was aiming for 'Dano-Norwegian', a name that pointed both to the point of departure (Danish) and the end goal of the programme (Norwegian). His approach to language planning was both original and creative. Today's Bokmål is very much the result of his ideas and his lifelong work. No other national standard in Europe has a history at all resembling that of Norwegian Bokmål in having been developed incrementally out of another language (cf. Kloss 1967).

Knudsen was also proud of the fact that he had published his proposal for a Norwegian language planning programme before Aasen made his own public. Knudsen referred to his own standard as embodying the slow evolutionary route, and not the rushed revolutionary path which in his view characterised Aasen's programme for a language standard, to which we will now turn.

IVAR AASEN (1813–96): 'NORWAY IS OLD'

Aasen completely dismissed upper-middle-class speech, the Dano-Norwegian creoloid, as a basis for the establishment of a national standard. He found this idiom to be too closely connected to Danish to be able to serve as a convincing linguistic symbol of the Norwegian nation. Instead, he designed his own research programme for studying rural dialects, with the ultimate goal of extracting from them a national linguistic standard. This would establish Norwegian (as he defined it) as an independent and separate language, with its own history, dialects and, most importantly, a written standard based on peasant dialects, which would be on a par with its well-established Scandinavian sister languages, Danish and Swedish. The thinking behind his work was both nationalistic (cf. Walton 1987: 179–88) and public-spirited; indeed, Aasen wrote that whatever he had accomplished had been done in order to aid the common people of Norway.

Biography

Ivar Aasen, born in 1813 into a peasant family in Ørsta in the western region of Sunnmøre, has become a national icon, although his iconic status is not accepted by everyone. His image is that of a smallholder farmer's son, an unassuming man who contributed immensely to the linguistic advancement of his country. However, although he was self-taught and lived in an extremely spartan manner all his life – and appeared poor from the way he dressed – Aasen was an intellectual who, once he reached adulthood, never had anything more to do with either farming or physical labour.

Aasen enjoyed a tremendous amount of authority during his lifetime as an academic and linguistic scholar, and he was elected Member of the Royal Norwegian Society of Sciences and Letters, founded in 1760 in Trondhjem (from 1931: Trondheim). He was awarded a medal of achievement by the Swedish-Norwegian king. However, when invited in 1857 to become one of the founding members of the Society of Science and Letters in Christiania (today: The Norwegian Academy of Science and Letters), Aasen turned this down. He also declined an offer to become a university professor.

While Aasen was shy and modest, for most of his life he belonged to the country's intellectual elite, lived in the capital and usually spoke the variety of the Norwegian upper-middle classes. He received an annual salary directly from Parliament from the early 1850s until his death in 1896. Like Knudsen, he remained a bachelor all his life, dedicating all his time and energy to his work (Venås 1996; Walton 1996; Grepstad 2013).

Aasen's programme from his 1836 essay

The philosophical basis for Ivar Aasen's work was National Romanticism, inspired by the ideas of the German philosopher Johann Gottfried Herder (1744–1803), who claimed that it was of the utmost importance for a nation to have its own language, and that this was the most prominent defining feature of a separate and independent country (cf. Walton 1987). Aasen argued that it was necessary after 1814 to build a national awareness of the fact that dialects within Norway had developed directly from Old Norse – independently of Danish – and that they constituted a separate branch of the Germanic and Nordic/Scandinavian languages.

The historical comparative linguistic theory developed by Rasmus Rask, Jacob Grimm and Franz Bopp served as an excellent tool for his endeavours, and Aasen exploited this approach in a very creative way when constructing his written standard based on contemporary peasant dialects. It was necessary to establish a direct historical relationship between modern nineteenth-century Norway and the Middle Ages, running through the centuries-long union with Denmark, by finding connections and concrete linguistic correlations. Aasen offered linguistic evidence for such links in his first major published works (1848, 1850), where he established that the modern dialects spoken by rural peasants could be described as having evolved directly from Old Norse, without taking Danish into account. This meant that the Danish period, during which the dialects in Norway had been considered dialects of Danish, could ultimately be disregarded. We can say that Aasen provided the linguistic evidence showing that the period of Danish domination was in reality an unimportant episode in the long history of Norwegian as a separate language.

In order to achieve his goal of connecting – through linguistic evidence – these two separate periods of Norwegian history, Aasen necessarily had to disregard any product of the language contact that had occurred during the Dano-Norwegian period. This meant that the Dano-Norwegian creoloid had to be excluded from consideration, even though it was the mother tongue of the upper-middle classes and had undoubtedly developed within the borders of Norway. A revolutionary sociolinguistic agenda emerged from this approach: the spoken idiom of the country's upper-middle classes was to be labelled irrelevant for the development of a national language standard.

As mentioned earlier, in 1832 the historian P. A. Munch intimated that a national written standard could be developed by selecting one of the more archaic rural dialects and then standardising it. This idea seemed better to Aasen than the Aall–Wergeland–Knudsen plan to Norwegianise Danish. Nevertheless, Aasen rejected the single-dialect solution, writing in 1836 that it would not be right to favour one dialect over the others, and that all dialects should in principle be included in the new standard. (This important paper was eventually published posthumously; see Aasen [1836] 1909.) Thus the grammar of the Norwegian national standard was not to be based on a single dialect but rather was to be abstracted from the shared systematic features that he expected to find when studying every accessible dialect. A national written standard could be based directly on the dialects while simultaneously being raised above them, because ideally the written form would not favour any particular dialect.

Aasen was very conscious of the sociopolitical and sociolinguistic aspects of his language programme, and emphasised both elements in his work. His programme was thus both nationalist and socially revolutionary in nature. The idea that the national language of Norway should act as a common denominator for all rural, low-status dialects, to the exclusion of the spoken variety of the upper-middle classes, has motivated thousands of people over the years to join the Landsmål/ Nynorsk movement in order to develop it and expand its use into new areas. Clearly, implementing Aasen's language programme in full as the sole national standard represented a fundamental sociolinguistic revolution.

Figure 3.2   Ivar Aasen (1813–96), photo. (Source: C. C. Wischmann/Archive Ivar Aasen-tunet.)

Fieldwork 1842–6

Between 1842 and 1846, Aasen travelled around Norway on a grant from the Royal Norwegian Society of Sciences and Letters. He studied dialects and collected material for a grammar and a dictionary of, as he called it, 'the Norwegian people's language' (*det norske folkesprog*).

His method was to select a central location in every area to which he travelled, as he felt it was better to stay for a long period of time in one place rather than try and cover as many locations as possible. Aasen managed to reach the majority of regions in southern Norway during his travels, getting as far north as Rana in the southern part of northern Norway. During his journeys, Aasen avoided the towns and cities, since he claimed that the language spoken there would be too greatly influenced by Danish.

Aasen ultimately settled in Christiania in 1847. However, to the extent that his health permitted, every summer he visited places that he had not been to during his initial period of fieldwork.

Grammar and Dictionary of the Norwegian People's Language (1848, 1850)

Aasen possessed an unusual ability to navigate through and systematise a vast linguistic corpus. However, he did not present his proposal for a new national written standard all at once.

First, he published the material collected during his 1842–6 fieldwork in two books, *The Grammar of the Norwegian People's Language* (*Det norske Folkesprogs Grammatik*, 1848) and *The Dictionary of the Norwegian People's Language* (*Ordbog over det norske Folkesprog*, 1850), in which he showed how the modern popular dialects he had investigated could be regarded as being related to, and indeed developed from, Old Norse. The grammar and dictionary were received with enthusiasm by the upper-middle-class intelligentsia. P. A. Munch wrote very positive reviews of Aasen's grammar (Munch 1848), and Aasen was hailed as the man who had documented the linguistic ties between ancient, medieval and modern Norway.

For the nationalist-oriented intelligentsia, Aasen had provided the proof that Norway was an ancient country. The fact that underlying this discovery was a sociolinguistic understanding of the linguistic situation that could serve as the basis for a revolutionary national language planning programme was not mentioned. Indeed, no one in the early 1850s – with the exception of Aasen himself – seems to have foreseen such a development.

The first Landsmaal standard: 1853

The next step in Aasen's plan was to establish a unifying standard, or a written 'expression' of all the various dialects, a project requiring several years of intensive work. It was only with the publication of his *Norwegian Grammar* (*Norsk Grammatik*, 1864) and *Norwegian Dictionary* (*Norsk Ordbog*, 1873) that we can claim that the 'Aasen Standard' was fully elaborated. However, Aasen launched a preliminary version as early as 1853, calling it Landsmaal, and we may therefore identify 1853 as the year of the birth of this new language standard.

Aasen's proposal appeared in his book *Samples of the Landsmaal in Norway* (*Prøver af Landsmaalet i Norge*, 1853). This work contains examples of rural dialects representing the whole country, thirty-two dialect texts in all. It was in the final section of this book that Aasen suggested his standard, Landsmaal, as a unifying pan-dialectal written standard for the dialects shown in the first part of the book. To illustrate the use of the standard, the final part of the book contained various texts written in the Landsmaal standard.

The various opinions as to whether the name Landsmaal referred to the language of the country or the language of the countryside made no sense to Aasen himself. Both views would be debated heavily over the following sixty to seventy years. As Aasen saw it, the idiom spoken in the towns was too greatly influenced by Danish to deserve inclusion in a truly national standard, so the language spoken in the countryside was the only possible basis for such a standard. According to Aasen, this constituted no contradiction. It was only at a much later stage – when it was discovered that the popular dialects of the towns and cities should also be considered 'good' Norwegian dialects 'untainted' by Danish (cf. Handagard 1901; Jahr 1984: 121–30) – that the term *Landsmaal* became inappropriate and attempts to change the term were initiated, leading ultimately to the introduction of the name *Nynorsk* in 1929.

The 'Aasen Standard': 1864, 1873

Four principles may be distinguished as having been especially important to Aasen in developing the Landsmaal standard:

1. There should be only one valid form of each word: a word was to be conjugated in one way only, and there were to be no optional parallel forms. This was a basic principle for Aasen. When we take into account the wide variety of forms that Aasen had found in the dialects, and reported on in his 1848 grammar, this principle was not easy to implement, and Aasen worked on this for many years before he arrived at the solutions he wanted.
2. The standard forms were to be based on contemporary spoken dialects. This principle implied that all elements of the standard had to be found in some contemporary dialect.
3. The standard should be uniform, consistent and logical; that is, words which were connected by meaning and etymology should reveal this connection in the way they were spelt.
4. Old Norse was considered to be the historical point of departure for contemporary dialects, thus being the final source to which to appeal when it became difficult to choose between different dialectal forms.

In the 1850s, Aasen worked on the Landsmaal standard in several stages before completing his final version (Haugen 1931), which is usually referred to as the 'Aasen Standard'. It was not an easy task, and it demanded the systematic genius of Aasen to construct a coherent grammatical system from all the various different dialect forms. He almost gave up at times. In 1859, he thought his grammar would be finished within a year. But it took much longer, and just the chapter about the declinations took a whole year to complete (Venås 1997: 156). When he finally published the second edition of his grammar in 1864 and of his dictionary in 1873, the trial-and-error period was over, and the final Aasen Standard was released to the public. (On the relationship between the first and second edition of Aasen's grammar, see Linn 1997.) The main points of the Aasen Standard may be summarised as follows:

1. Nouns are declined in the masculine, feminine (strong and weak) and neuter genders. (Danish, in comparison, had two genders

– common and neuter – the same as in upper-middle-class Norwegian speech.)

The masculine gender, for example:
ein gard – garden – gardar – gardarne
'a farm – the farm – farms – the farms'

The feminine gender, for example:
(Note: strong feminine nouns end either in a consonant or are monosyllablic (for example, *bygd* 'parish', *ku* 'cow'), while weak feminine nouns end in *-a* in the indefinite singular, for example *visa* 'song'.)
strong nouns: *ei bygd – bygdi – bygder – bygderna*
'a parish – the parish – parishes – the parishes'
weak nouns: *ei visa – visa – visor – visorna*
'a song – the song – songs – the songs'

The neuter gender, for example:
eit fjell – fjellet – fjell – fjelli
'a mountain – the mountain – mountains – the mountains'

2. Conjugation of verbs:
The infinitive ending is *-a* (Danish and upper-middle-class speech used *-e*).

Weak verbs of the 1st conjugation, for example:
aa kasta – kastar – kastade – kastat
'to throw – throws – threw – thrown'
(As we saw earlier, Danish had the ending *-ede*, in the past tense, for example *kastede*, while upper-middle-class Norwegian speech used *-et*, a form found exclusively in that variety and in the Bergen city dialect, for example *kastet*; cf. Jahr 2001, 2012.)

Strong verbs, for example:
aa skriva – skriv – skreiv – skrivet
'to write – writes – wrote – written'
(cf. *at skrive – skriver – skrev – skrevet* in Danish and upper-middle-class speech)

3. Personal pronouns, subject and object cases:
eg – meg ('I – me'; Dan. *jeg – mig*),
du – deg ('you – you'; Dan. *du – dig*),

han – honom ('he – him'; Dan. *han – ham*),
ho – henne ('she – her'; Dan. *hun – hende*),
det – det ('it – it'; Dan. *det – det*)
me – oss ('we – us'; Dan. *vi – oss*),
de – dykk ('you – you'; Dan. *I – Eder*),
dei – deim ('they – them'; Dan. *de – dem*)

4. The use of diphthongs was very salient in the Aasen Standard (instead of the monophthongs of Danish and, in most cases, upper-middle-class speech), as were distinctive forms such as *bljug* ('modest, shy'; Dan. *blyg*), *sjo* ('sea'; Dan. *søe*), *snjo* ('snow'; Dan. *snee*), *kvat* ('what'; Dan. *hvad*), *nokot* ('something'; Dan. *noget*) and *deild* ('part', noun; Dan. *deel*).

It has been claimed that the principle inherent in Aasen's Standard is 'democratic', in that he based it not on a single dialect but on all the existing rural dialects. It is difficult to imagine that P. A. Munch's proposal to construct a national standard from one dialect alone would have aroused the interest and enthusiasm of people all around the country to the same extent that Aasen's democratic principle has succeeded in doing ever since the 1850s.

A major feature of his Landsmaal standard was its lexically purity. Aasen did not want to include in his standard any obviously Danish and Low German loan words, especially those with the prefixes *an-* (for example, *anta* 'assume') and *be-* (for example, *begynne* 'begin') and with the suffices *-hed* (for example, *nyhed* 'news') and *-else* (for example, *antagelse* 'assumption'). The fundamental rationale for this purism was Aasen's ambition to demonstrate the direct linguistic link between Old Norse and the modern peasant dialects. If all the clearly Danish and Low German loan words – which had been borrowed during the Dano-Norwegian union – were kept out of the written standard, this historical connection would stand out more saliently. Later, especially in the nineteenth century, another motivation was added to defend this puristic tradition: the Danish and Low German loan words belonged to and 'invited' writers to use a style alien to the oral style favoured in Landsmål/Nynorsk (Gerdener 1986).

Over the years, assessments of the Aasen Standard have differed quite considerably. Many people have been struck by its thorough and systematic structure. Every part of it is well conceived and considered, and all elements appear to be in the right place. It is easy to demonstrate that the principle of constructing the standard from modern dialects permeates the entire nature of his work.

However, many others have claimed that the standard suggested by Aasen was too old-fashioned and thus difficult to use from the very beginning. Some people believe that, while developing the standard, Aasen allowed himself to become too greatly influenced by Old Norse. This is not correct: Aasen followed his four principles, and these drove him to introduce older, more archaic dialect forms into his standard. However, these forms were all still found in some dialect. What Aasen suggested was a kind of proto-Norwegian derived from the contemporary peasant dialects by employing the methods of historical comparative linguistics.

It is nevertheless clear that an inherent contradiction existed between, on the one hand, Aasen's wish to create a written standard for the common people – for those who had the least time available for schooling and practical writing instruction – and, on the other hand, the result of the methods and principles he chose to use in elaborating the standard. This contradiction was the source of the markedly different opinions within and outside the Landsmaal language movement as to how successful the Aasen Standard was as a written language for the majority of people. It is also quite obvious that the puristic tradition initiated by Aasen has been an obstacle for many people over the years.

Aasen's followers agreed with him about ignoring upper-middle-class speech when constructing the standard, since they regarded this as Danish. In their view, only the rural peasant dialects represented a 'true' national linguistic core on which to build the standard. It was also an important consideration for them that speakers of these rural dialects, taken together, greatly outnumbered users of upper-middle-class speech. However, as Knudsen argued, the Dano-Norwegian creoloid without doubt had many more speakers than any single rural dialect. When Aasen produced what many considered to be compelling evidence that all dialects constituted a single linguistic system which could be called 'Norwegian', this fact could be used to declare Knudsen's claim null and void. Ultimately, the number of speakers of 'Norwegian' – as defined by Aasen – was by far larger than the number of Dano-Norwegian creoloid speakers.

The view of most Norwegian linguists who have worked in the field of Nordic/Scandinavian linguistics is that Ivar Aasen discovered and demonstrated the unity and internal systematicity of the Norwegian popular dialects, and it was on this basis that he formulated his proposal for the Landsmaal standard. Thus, in principle, so the claim goes, Aasen based his standard on *all* the rural dialects. However, one can turn this statement around and claim that Aasen's work created an *apparent* unity among the many diverse Norwegian dialects so that they could serve his linguistic and nationalistic purposes. This, of course, was the view held by many of Aasen's opponents.

As a result of his comprehensive fieldwork covering most parts of the country, and of his language planning efforts (cf. Aasen 1848, 1850, 1853, 1864, 1873), Norwegian – as Aasen defined it – was by 1875 one of the best described languages in the world, according to Einar Haugen (1965).

The theory of the 'two cultures'

Aasen was not alone in providing folk material which pointed to the distant past. Asbjørnsen and Moe's collection of fairytales, and the collection of legends and folk ballads also contributed to this.

However, it was Aasen's work that was utilised in a national political campaign outlining the programme for establishing a truly Norwegian national standard. In this campaign, Aasen promoted a historical interpretation of what should be considered 'Norwegian', of who represented 'Norsedom' (that is, the peasants), and of how the spoken variety that had developed during the Dano-Norwegian union (the Dano-Norwegian creoloid, upper-middle-class speech) was to be assessed in a national context.

From Aasen's basic understanding and analysis there was only a short path to the idea that there was one national and one foreign culture in competition in Norway, a claim which has been referred to as the theory of the 'two cultures' (Garborg 1877). The Danish language and culture, as embodied in the upper-middle classes, represented the foreign and colonial, whereas the indigenous culture resided exclusively in the peasants and ordinary people. This rivalry between these two cultures was expressed in the peasants' political opposition to the ruling upper-middle classes. Gradually, the Aasen Standard came to be seen as a threat to the linguistic privileges of the ruling class. Launching attacks against the language hegemony exercised by the upper-middle classes became an important tactic of the political opposition, and Aasen's Landsmaal emerged as something concrete which the opposition could argue for and promote.

TWO OPPOSING SOCIOLINGUISTIC PROGRAMMES OF LANGUAGE PLANNING

Knud Knudsen and Ivar Aasen were diametrically opposed in their assessments of what should be considered 'Norwegian', even though both took contemporary spoken language in Norway as their point of departure. Knudsen wanted to expand on the language of the upper-middle classes, the societal elite, who had fostered independence in 1814 and who were politically and culturally dominant in the new nation, while Aasen used the popular dialects of peasants to forge a link to the country's Norse past. The sociolinguistic difference between the two standards that emerged as the result of their proposals proved to be decisive for the linguistic development of modern Norway. The county's language conflict in the nineteenth and twentieth centuries was based primarily on this sociolinguistic difference, albeit often masked by nationalist rhetoric.

Landsmaal had its social base among the peasants, who early in the nineteenth century represented approximately 95 per cent of the Norwegian population. The social background of Dano-Norwegian speakers was the upper-middle classes, who were a small minority. However, the growing class of workers in the towns and cities, especially from the early twentieth century onwards, was not very much inclined to support the use of Landsmaal. Its image as a rural standard was probably the most important factor behind this, since the working classes most often identified with a more urban way of life, which included using, as they saw it, an urban language variety. This fact makes it impossible to claim that there was simply an opposition between the low social class (Landsmaal) and the upper-middle class (Dano-Norwegian, later Riksmål).

Despite the social basis of his language programme, Knudsen did not receive a great deal of support from the upper-middle classes. It may appear as something of a paradox that Aasen's work, on the other hand, did win their approval. However, there is nothing strange about this. The most important result of Aasen's first two books was the historical link he demonstrated between Norwegian dialects and Old

Norse. This contributed significantly to the view that the Norwegian nation had what many would claim were long and proud traditions dating back to the Old Norse period when, especially in the thirteenth century, Norway was a major regional power with considerable European influence. Since the upper-middle classes were strongly influenced by National Romanticism, they were also interested in these traditions.

But the elite was not prepared for the political consequences of these ideas, which would form the basis of an agrarian opposition movement that was motivated by the view that only the peasants were the bearers and saviours of Norwegian culture and traditions. The elite could not know – or believe – that Aasen's programme would be adopted and turned into a political project in the 1870s and 1880s which would be directed against upper-middle-class culture and used in the struggle against the ruling classes.

In the National Romantic fashion, the elite was enthusiastic about the rediscovery of fairytales and other popular folk traditions, and the peasant dialects belonged to this context without question. But most of the upper-middle classes did not see any reason for their written standard to be reformed, even though it was in essence the standard of a different country. On the contrary, in their view, their written standard represented civilised culture as well as education. Only when the Landsmaal project became an imminent threat as a result of the political developments of the 1870s and 1880s did Knudsen's language programme finally become more acceptable to the upper-middle classes.

Norwegian linguists following in Aasen's footsteps

Throughout the nineteenth century and well into the twentieth century, most Norwegian linguists working in Scandinavian/Nordic linguistics were primarily occupied with historical perspectives. Their theoretical underpinnings harked back to Jacob Grimm and other pioneers of the historical comparative period, a time when National Romantic philosophy dominated both the German arena and other countries influenced by German culture. Using the Neogrammarian approach (based, among other things, on Hermann Paul's seminal work, *Prinzipen der Sprachgeschichte* [1880]), most Norwegian linguists wanted to follow up Aasen's work by establishing historically sound principles which indicated the direct development from Old Norwegian/Norse to the modern dialects of Norway. In this context, all influence from Danish – whether in writing or speech – was of no scientific interest to them, as it was only a distraction from their main focus – the 'phonetic laws' connecting the old and the new Norway by means of language.

One obvious objective for them was that 'Norwegian', however it was defined, could be studied in Norway in the same way that, for example, Swedish could be studied in Sweden, and Polish in Poland. Three postulated relationships showing the direct connection to Aasen's analysis and programme highlight the basic assumptions that underpinned their approach: (1) the historical relationship between Old Norwegian/Norse and contemporary local dialects (first described in Aasen 1848 and 1850); (2) Aasen's claim that there is a systematic relationship between – in principal – all the rural dialects of the country (as described in Aasen 1864 and 1873); and (3) Aasen's assertion that his suggested written Landsmaal standard was the codification of the system inherent in all rural dialects (cf. Aasen 1853). So in order to pursue their historical-comparative approach more consistently, Norwegian linguists drew on the work of Aasen to justify their way of discriminating between different types of observed linguistic data: for them, acceptable synchronic data were simply those that could be related to Old Norwegian/Norse through Neogrammarian phonetic laws, while upper-middle-class speech in Norway, the Dano-Norwegian creoloid, would inevitably continue to be classified as 'non-Norwegian' or 'Danish'.

After Aasen's time, and up until the 1970s, a majority of the Norwegian linguists involved in studying Norwegian accepted this binary opposition in which a 'national' linguistic variety in principle had to be subsumed under the label of either Danish or Norwegian, with no third possibility. Since word forms and morphology in the Dano-Norwegian creoloid were derived from written Danish, the conclusion was that this variety had to be classified as Danish, regardless of the fact that its prosody and phonology were clearly non-Danish.

CHAPTER 4

The language question becomes a major political issue: 1860–1907

Political developments from 1845 to 1905

The main political issues in Norway in the second half of the nine-teenth century were the troubled relationship with Sweden – leading ultimately to the dissolution of their union in 1905 – followed by the change to parliamentary rule, together with an increase in the number of people given the right to vote in local and national elections (in 1897 suffrage was extended to all men, and in 1913 to all women). Political parties were slow to emerge in Norway as compared with other European countries. The Liberal Party (*Venstre*/'Left', which was against the union with Sweden) and the Conservative Party (*Høire*/'Right') were both established in 1884, and the Labour Party followed in 1887.

However, the Labour movement had much earlier origins. Inspired partly by the 1848 wave of revolutions in Europe, the Norwegian teacher, journalist and author Marcus Thrane (1817–90) initiated a protest movement in 1849 which was supported by working-class people in large parts of the country. At its peak, the movement con-sisted of almost 400 local associations with a total membership of close to 30,000. Thrane himself was arrested in 1851 and was convicted of being involved in subversive activities. He spent seven years in jail. Having their leader incarcerated shortened the local organisations' lifespan, but the Labour movement and Labour Party continued to take their inspiration from Thrane's movement (Bjørklund 1970; Pryser 1993).

The division of power between Parliament, the government and the judiciary laid out in the 1814 Constitution meant that until the introduction of parliamentary rule in 1884, the government operated much more independently than it could afterwards. Following several years of fierce political battles, the opposition – headed by the Liberal Party – toppled the government, and with it the old regime, which was supported by the Conservative Party. The rather dramatic events of 1884 (including the impeachment of the entire government) have been described as a bloodless coup. The opposition seized power and permanently established the principle of parliamentary rule. Ivar Aasen's language project was perfectly suited to this fight against the government and the upper-middle-class establishment, since Landsmaal was seen as the written manifestation of the peasant dialects, while upper-middle-class speech was 'not Norwegian'.

Competition between Landsmaal and Danish starts in 1858; the first Landsmaal organisations

When the poet and journalist Aasmund Olavsson Vinje (1818–70) switched from writing in Danish to using Landsmaal in 1858, and in the same year launched a weekly Landsmaal magazine called *Dølen* (*The Dalesman*), this represented the first example of competition between Danish (soon Dano-Norwegian) and the emerging Landsmaal standard devised by Aasen. At this point, Landsmaal was still in its early stages of development, as we have seen. When Vinje started writing in Landsmaal, he was therefore necessarily using the provisional standard proposed by Aasen in 1853, though also relying quite heavily on his own native Telemark dialect.

The first Landsmaal organisations which were to prove lasting were Det Norske Samlaget (The Norwegian Association) in Kristiania and Vestmannalaget (The Westerners' Association) in Bergen (Haugland 1981; Hoel 2011: 29ff.), both of which were founded in 1868 in the midst of the political tensions in the country. A conflict connected to the so-called 'Second Union Committee', which had proposed that the ties between Norway and Sweden should be strengthened, influenced the entire political scene. From their rather slow organisational start in the late 1860s, local Landsmaal Societies (*Maallag*) eventually emerged all over the country. By 1892, there were probably around thirty of them working actively in their local communities. By

1905, the number had increased to around one hundred, and by that time they had also organised themselves into County Associations (*Fylkesmaallag*), eleven of which were in operation around 1905 (Haugland 1971a, 1977a: 19). The next obvious organisational move would be to establish a nationwide association, which happened in 1906 (Haugland 1970).

From the very beginning the organised sector of the Landsmaal movement was closely tied to a national, anti-Swedish-union policy, and was thus allied with the Liberal Party. However, from the outset the movement was motivated by both nationalist and pro-democracy sentiments; and it turned out that different supporters tended to put more emphasis on one or other of these aspects, which led to conflicts, so language activists ended up adopting different strategies in their political-linguistic work (V. Skard 1949).

Until 1905, the strength of the more nationally oriented and more socially oriented groups within the Landsmaal movement was evenly balanced, because the national and social struggles coincided with the general political struggle against the ruling elite in Norway. In both respects, the peasant movement faced the same adversary – government officials of the old regime, who were both generally in favour of maintaining the union with Sweden and opposed to democratic developments in society. These officials often sided politically with the Conservative Party and were against the rise of Landsmaal. Having a common enemy thus held the various groups within the Landsmaal movement together.

Landsmaal becomes a major political issue

Aasen's linguistic project, then, became part of a national political programme adopted by the peasant opposition and the Liberal Party. Their platform supported the official establishment of an exclusively Norwegian written standard as part of their anti-unionist view of Norway's continually problematic relationship with Sweden. So Landsmaal proved to be important in two central political respects. First, it provided a way of attacking the ruling classes, and the entire old regime, on nationalist grounds. But it was also a tool for developing a new cultural and social sense of self-esteem among the rural population on whose dialects it was built, as well as a means of stimulating cultural and literary activities in rural areas (cf. Garborg 1877).

The advocates of Landsmaal in Parliament thus used arguments which can be labelled democratic, pedagogic and national, the last reflecting National Romantic ideas. They reasoned that it was democratic and pedagogically advantageous to favour a written standard based on the spoken language of the majority of the population. Moreover, this was nationally important and necessary, since an independent nation needed a written language of its own, and the majority of the population – the peasants – represented all that was genuinely Norwegian.

The opponents of Landsmaal in Parliament could hardly disagree with the pedagogical line of reasoning; instead, they argued that the dialects differed from each other so much linguistically that they could not be said to be better represented in the Landsmaal of Aasen than in the Dano-Norwegian standard. Dano-Norwegian was uniform, while Landsmaal was obviously still at a trial-and-error phase; and Dano-Norwegian conveyed culture and breeding. Politically speaking, it proved impossible for them to oppose the general national arguments marshalled by the supporters of Landsmaal. However, Landsmaal's opponents claimed that only the actual dialects represented national values, and not Aasen's 'constructed' Landsmaal standard itself.

Many of Aasen's supporters, headed by Liberal Party Chairman Johan Sverdrup (1816–92), considered the various local dialects and the Landsmaal standard as being in principle one coherent language. Supporting the use of the local peasant dialects and Landsmaal was therefore viewed by Sverdrup and the Liberals as two sides of the same national and democratic cause (Haugland 1974). The tactics of Landsmaal's opponents were to establish that there was an incompatibility between Landsmaal and the dialects: they claimed that they were in favour of the dialects and their use, but opposed Landsmaal because they rejected the claim that this standard could serve as a better written expression of the dialects than could the Dano-Norwegian standard.

A breakthrough for Aasen's definition of 'Norwegian': oral instruction in schools (1878)

Aasen, his followers and the political opposition in Parliament regarded the rural dialects as the only true oral manifestation of the Norwegian language, as they had survived the 400–year period of union with

Denmark. This view called for a policy of supporting and stimulating the use of these dialects, both in society at large and in schools in particular. The alternative to speaking dialect in schools would be to introduce a spoken standard; and the only serious candidate for this was the Dano-Norwegian creoloid, because it had the necessary social status and was closer to written Dano-Norwegian. In addition, it was used all over the country by the upper-middle classes and was more or less understood everywhere, or so the claim went. But for those individuals who supported Landsmaal and agreed that the creoloid was in principle Danish, the introduction of a spoken standard in the schools was not an option at all.

In 1878, Parliament passed a resolution stating that oral instruction in primary schools should be based on the dialects of the pupils. The following year, the government changed the instructions for schools to reflect this view (Jahr 1984: 51). The Landsmaal movement had won its first major political victory. All later decisions and political progress for the Landsmaal cause were founded on this ground-breaking principle, which is still in operation today: schoolchildren throughout the country use and – as far as possible – receive instruction in their own local dialect.

An important breakthrough for Knudsen's ideas: reading pronunciation in schools (1887)

In 1887, Knudsen's programme received an important boost when the Ministry of Church and Education accepted one of Knudsen's main points: that there was – or ought to be – a close correspondence between everyday spoken language and the written standard (Knudsen 1861). The Ministry sent out a circular informing schools that the model for reading aloud should be 'cultivated daily speech' (*dannet dagligtale*), that is, upper-middle-class speech. This put an end to the unnatural spelling pronunciation of the written Danish standard which had long been practised in schools (cf. Jonas Anton Hielm's third 'dialect'). However, the decision created other problems because there were great differences between the written language (Dano-Norwegian) and upper-middle-class speech, which was now to be the norm for reading aloud in classrooms.

This situation had, of course, long been foreseen by Knudsen. The new difficulties obviously helped prepare the ground for a reform of the Dano-Norwegian written standard under the linguistic influence of the upper-middle-class oral variety. Knudsen had achieved two important steps that were necessary for implementing his programme of developing a written standard that reflected this variety in phonology, morphology and lexicon. The first was the 1862 Orthographic Reform, which secured the important principle that the written standard would be developed independently in Norway without reference to Danish. The second step was this 1887 government circular, making the cultivated daily speech of the upper-middle classes the norm for the reading standard.

Parliament's 1878 resolution about oral instruction in primary schools meant that the 1887 norm for reading texts aloud was not to be confused with the language of instruction. However, the discrepancy between schoolchildren's dialects (the language of instruction), upper-middle-class speech (the norm for reading aloud), and spelling (still Danish, except for the 1862 changes in orthography) – along with many schoolteachers' and pupils' lack of experience in using the upper-middle-class oral variety – all paved the way for urgent changes to the written Dano-Norwegian standard. For example, words written like *fader* and *moder* ('father' and 'mother') were supposed to be pronounced /faːr/ and /muːr/, verbs spelt as *lade* and *sige* ('let' and 'say') were to be pronounced /laː/ and /siː/, and the nouns *bogen* and *æblet* ('the book' and 'the apple') were to be read aloud as /buːkn/ and /eple/; these upper-middle-class pronunciations created severe problems for teachers and schoolchildren alike.

It was probably not possible to implement the 1887 resolution in the schools. However, it was extremely important for Knudsen's programme to have the principle acknowledged that when the written standard was read aloud in Norway, it was to be pronounced using a spoken variety found within the boundaries of the country.

Language Equality Resolution (1885)

The advance of Landsmaal required important political decisions to be taken, and those who directly opposed Landsmaal were in a minority in Parliament during the 1870s, 1880s and 1890s. The 1878 resolution about oral instruction in schools provided the basis for the Language Equality Resolution (*Jamstillingsvedtaket*), in which the two written standards, Dano-Norwegian and Landsmaal, were officially declared equal. On 12 May 1885, Parliament passed the following resolution, with seventy-eight members voting in favour and thirty-one against:

> The Government is requested to ensure that the necessary measures are taken so that the Norwegian Folk Language [*det norske Folkesprog*] as a language for schools and official use be given equal status with our usual written language and book language [i.e., Dano-Norwegian]. (Jahr 1994: 21; author's translation.)

During the Parliamentary discussions on this issue, some Members of Parliament made efforts to include Knudsen's programme in the decision, which caused some confusion towards the end of the debate. It has been much disputed since then whether the Language Equality Resolution embraced both Aasen's Landsmaal and Knudsen's agenda; supporters of Landsmaal have mostly refuted this interpretation, while supporters of Riksmaal have favoured it. What is important, however, is not an isolated semantic analysis of the debate and the wording of the resolution, but how the decision was followed up politically. There can be no doubt that the resolution was of particular importance for the Landsmaal movement, but the fact that Knudsen was ultimately brought into the discussion proved that the climate was definitely improving for his language planning programme as well (Bull 1987; Jahr and Schanche 1988; Hoel 2011: 73ff.).

The Language Equality Resolution was a tremendous victory for Aasen's Landsmaal programme and also for the Liberal Party government. To the upper-middle classes – the establishment and supporters of the old political regime that had lost power in 1884 – the 1885 resolution which gave the two standards equal status was an omen of what was to come on the sociolinguistic scene. A fundamental sociolinguistic revolution – from below – was a definite possibility.

Language Paragraph Amendment to the School Act (1892)

The 1885 resolution on language equality was later used to argue for inserting a special language paragraph (*maalparagrafen*) in the School Act. But when a new School Act was passed by Parliament in 1889, this paragraph did not achieve the necessary majority support. However, three years later Parliament amended the Act to include a paragraph empowering local school boards throughout the country to decide which of the two varieties (Dano-Norwegian or Landsmaal) pupils were to have as their written standard, and thus which standard their schoolbooks would be written in.

Parliament's decision to place both standards on an equal footing was thus finally incorporated into the School Act in 1892. An additional clause stated that pupils were to learn to read both standards. Thus, in 1892 the Landsmaal movement acquired the necessary legal basis for setting out to win over the school districts for their cause.

The importance of Landsmaal authors Aasen, Blix, Vinje and Garborg

To successfully develop and spread Aasen's version of Landsmaal as a written standard, it was necessary for authors to start employing it, and, most importantly, to show the public both that it *could* be used and also *how* it could be used in various written genres. The four most important authors in this respect were Ivar Aasen himself, Elias Blix, Aasmund Olavsson Vinje and Arne Garborg.

Aasen realised early on that it was imperative for people to be able to see the Landsmaal standard in actual use. Consequently, he wrote a play – *The Heir* (*Ervingen*) – which was staged in April 1855; it was the first play in which all the actors (with one exception) spoke Landsmaal. Later, Aasen published a book of poems in Landsmaal (1863, final edition 1875), as well as a book for young people covering different aspects of society and science (1875), with some chapters devoted to language and dialects. This book represents the first attempt to develop specifically Norwegian terminology for several fields of study. Aasen's book of poems (or songs, as he liked to call them) became very popular; even today several of the songs from both this book and *The Heir* are widely known and sung.

Elias Blix (1836–1902) was a university professor of Hebrew and Bible Studies, as well as a member of the Liberal Party government from 1884 onwards. He penned many hymns in Landsmaal, and he also translated large sections of the Bible into the new standard. He started to publish his hymns in 1869 (Blix 1869), and soon many parishes wanted to use them in church, a wish that was officially granted in 1892 by the Ministry of Church and Education (Hoel 2011: 142). With Lutheranism being the state religion, as stated in the

1814 Constitution, all regulations concerning the Church – including sermons, the hymn book and additional hymns – had to be authorised by the Ministry. Aasen had thought that the religious sphere would be the most resistant to the new standard and thus the most difficult to win over. However, he was proved wrong (Tvinnereim 1973; Furre 1997; Bull 2002), and a major reason for Landsmaal's early conquest of the Church and religious life in general was clearly Blix's popular hymns. Many of these are still in use today, and one has become Norway's national hymn. (The lyrics of the national *anthem* were written by Bjørnstjerne Bjørnson in 1859 [Lomheim 2007: 302f.].)

The poems of Aasmund Olavsson Vinje (1818–70) are also still sung today, having been put to the music of Edvard Grieg. Vinje's main contribution to the development of Landsmaal, however, was in the field of journalism. He is widely considered as one of the country's foremost journalists, and he demonstrated through his writings that the new standard could be used for whatever subject he wanted to cover. Vinje's early switch from Dano-Norwegian to Landsmaal, as far back as 1858, has been described as something of a linguistic redemption, liberating his talent as a writer and poet (cf. Waschnitius 1921).

The last of the four men who were most important for the proliferation of Landsmaal in the final half of the nineteenth century was Arne Garborg (1851–1924) (cf. Elswijk 2010). He was without doubt the person who contributed the most to developing Landsmaal from a more-or-less theoretical concept to a written standard that could be used successfully in numerous fields (Dale 1950). Garborg wrote on an impressive range of topics from the 1870s onwards and convincingly demonstrated that the new national standard could be used just as effectively as Dano-Norwegian, in which he also frequently wrote and published.

Garborg started out as a journalist and was the founder, editor and main contributor to the Landsmaal weekly magazine which succeeded Vinje's *The Dalesman*, which folded when Vinje died in 1870. The new magazine, *The Ancestral Home* (*Fedraheimen*), was published between 1877 and 1891, and Garborg served as its editor until 1882. Garborg followed Vinje's lead in journalism and proved that Landsmaal could be used to good effect when describing and discussing politics, society, culture and art. He also published novels, plays and poetry using this new standard. Later, he turned to classical works and translated Homer's *The Odyssey* into Landsmaal (Garborg 1918),

Figure 4.1   Arne Garborg (1851–1924), photo. (Source: unknown/National Library of Norway.)

the first translation of *The Odyssey* to appear in Norwegian. From the 1880s onwards, Garborg was an esteemed European literary figure, and his novels were translated into several major European languages. Garborg was nominated several times as a serious contender for the Nobel Prize in Literature.

Together, these four authors developed the Landsmaal standard and employed it for different genres, styles and topics. In essence, they turned the orthographic, morphological and lexical standard suggested by Aasen into a literary standard which was flexible in syntax and style. Moreover, in this endeavour they used oral language as their model, thus moving the standard away from the more complicated literary style of written Danish. This oral style was later seen as an integral part of the Landsmaal standard. Landsmaal was built up from the spoken dialects, and its syntax and style were to be in keeping with this oral basis.

The first officially authorised Landsmaal standard

Throughout the 1890s, Landsmaal was introduced as the main written standard in quite a large number of school districts. Between 1892 and 1900, around 250 school districts opted for Landsmaal, and from 1900 to 1905 another one hundred and seventy were added (Hovdan 1947: 94). It had obviously become necessary to establish an officially recognised standard (the Aasen Standard had never been officially accepted). In a circular distributed to schools in 1893, the Ministry of Church and Education pointed to five books published in Landsmaal, declaring that the language used in them was to be the basis for future writing. This was not an optimal solution, because these five books did not show total agreement about certain linguistic forms, and many people wanted more consistency from a standard at that time.

The Ministry appointed a special three-member committee in 1898 to discuss the issue. It consisted of Marius Hægstad (1850–1927), who was appointed to the first Chair of Landsmaal at the University of Kristiania in 1899, Arne Garborg and Rasmus Flo (1851–1905), the editor of the Landsmaal journal *Syn og Segn* from 1894. These three submitted their report in 1899 (Hægstad et al. 1899), and in 1901 the Ministry authorised the 'Hægstad Standard'. Garborg and Flo recommended a number of further, quite substantial, changes to the Aasen Standard, greatly expanding on the inclusion of mountain dialects from the southeastern valleys. Their suggestion came to be called the 'Midland Standard' (*Midlandsnormalen*), and in 1901 the Ministry permitted its use by schoolchildren. Garborg himself subsequently edited all his books in line with this standard; later on in the twentieth century other prominent authors used this unique Landsmaal variety in their writing. However, the main 1901 Landsmaal standard deviated far less from the Aasen Standard than Garborg and Flo wanted, following Professor Hægstad's recommendations (Venås 1992a: 296–309).

The most important changes instigated by the Hægstad Standard with respect to the Aasen Standard were:

1. Weak verbs of the 1st conjugation were to be declined in -*a* in both the past tense and the past participle, in contrast with -*ade* and -*ad*/-*at* in the Aasen Standard. With this change, the infinitive, the past tense and the past participle all ended in -*a*:
   The Aasen Standard: *kasta* – *kastar* (= present tense) – *kastade* – *kastat* > The Hægstad Standard: *kasta* – *kastar* – *kasta* – *kasta* ('throw – throws – threw – thrown').

2. -*t* was dropped in the past participle of strong verbs, for example *faret* > *fare* ('gone'), *komet* > *kome* ('come'), *skrivet* > *skrive* ('written'), as well as in word forms like *kvat* > *kva* ('what'), *nokot* > *noko* ('some'), *annat* > *anna* ('other').

3. Some individual words were given a new spelling, for example *snjo* > *snø* ('snow'), *sjo* > *sjø* ('sea'), *braud* > *brød* ('bread'), *deild* > *del* ('part'), *vin* > *ven* ('friend'), *dyrr* > *dør* ('door').

4. The capitalisation of nouns was abolished.

In sum, the Hægstad Standard rendered Landsmaal in a more modern form, one that was definitely closer to contemporary dialect speech. However, Aasen's principle stating that each grammatical category or feature ought to be clearly identifiable had to be compromised in order to achieve this change (cf. the weak 1st conjugation verb forms).

Landsmaal made compulsory in teacher training colleges (1902) and required for the high-school exam (1907)

Starting with the 1878 resolution on oral instruction in schools, the Landsmaal movement won a series of seminal political victories:

the Language Equality Resolution (1885), the Language Paragraph Amendment to the School Act (1892), Blix's Landsmaal hymns being authorised for use in church (1892), the first law written in Landsmaal passed by Parliament (1894), the option of using Landsmaal in one of the two native-language essays in the high-school exam (1896), the appointment of the first Professor of Landsmaal at the University of Kristiania (1899), and compulsory Landsmaal classes in teacher training colleges (1902) (Haugland 1985).

The 1902 resolution that individuals who wanted to become schoolteachers had to study and pass an exam in Landsmaal at teacher training college was the first that made Landsmaal obligatory for any group. The Landsmaal cause was strongly supported by many teachers; for instance, from 1897 to 1901, the number of students at teacher training colleges who opted for Landsmaal as their main written standard increased from 8 per cent to 31 per cent.

The fact that so many teachers actively supported and propagated the Landsmaal standard was very important, including in a political sense. Along with clergymen and physicians, teachers were typically leading citizens in their local communities. They were quite often elected onto local school boards, frequently serving as the chairman. Many of them went on to be elected as Members of Parliament. Without the massive support of so many schoolteachers all over the country, the political victories won for Landsmaal in Parliament and in local school districts would hardly have been possible (Haugland 1977b).

The main reason for teachers' strong support of Landsmaal is to be found in the social background of the majority of the male teachers. These men were gifted sons of peasants who were less interested in farming than in reading and studying. (Ivar Aasen himself came from such a background.) These young men did not attend high school in the towns and cities – high schools were more for the urban middle and upper classes; rather, they flocked to the local teacher training colleges which had been established in every diocese in the countryside from the late 1820s onwards. These colleges provided students with two years of training, after which graduates were certified to teach all subjects in primary school. Arne Garborg attended such a college in Agder on the south coast from 1868–70; however, he proved to be a rather ungifted teacher and soon turned to journalism and literature instead.

Every decision in favour of Landsmaal prior to 1902 had a clear optional element to it; that is, those who wanted to had the possibility of choosing to use Landsmaal instead of Dano-Norwegian. Until the 1902 regulation, no one was obliged to use Landsmaal if they did not wish to do so. Some opponents of Landsmaal regarded this new ruling as a warning sign and a bad omen of what was to come, fearing it would be followed by further pro-Landsmaal political decisions. They began to caution others against what they termed 'Landsmaal coercion' (*landsmaalstvangen*). This obviously strengthened the antagonism between the two factions, and the two sides soon became almost bitter enemies as increasingly harsher words were exchanged.

The next important pro-Landsmaal ruling came five years later in 1907 (Haugland 1971b) when Parliament decided that all high-school students had to write an essay in Landsmaal in order to pass their examinations. The native-language exam consisted of three essays for most of the candidates, two long ones written in their main standard (almost always Dano-Norwegian/Riksmaal), and one short essay in the other standard. However, students who chose to write one of the long essays in Landsmaal were exempted from the shorter third essay, since they had already proven their proficiency in both standards.

From Dano-Norwegian to Riksmaal, the 1907 language reform

In the 1850s and 1860s, written Danish in Norway differed lexically somewhat from the Danish written in Denmark. This is evidenced by the fact that the Danish priest and author Andreas Listov (1817–89) considered it useful to publish a relatively extensive collection of words (between 3,000 and 3,500) found in modern Norwegian literature after 1842 (Listov 1866) which were unknown in Denmark, or which had a different meaning or use in Denmark than in Norway. The book was meant as a guide for Danish readers of contemporary Norwegian literature.

Quite a number of the lexical items in the book were taken from published work by the Landsmaal poet Aasmund Olavsson Vinje, but most were found in the writings of authors who used Danish (or Dano-Norwegian): the fairytale collectors Peter Christen Asbjørnsen and Jørgen Moe, Bjørnstjerne Bjørnson, Henrik Ibsen, Henrik Wergeland, and others. This is a clear indication that Norwegian

Figure 4.2   Bjørnstjerne Bjørnson (1832–1910), photo. (Source: Gustav Borgen/ National Library of Norway.)

poets and authors had used Danish in such a way that it now differed somewhat from the Danish used in Denmark. Asbjørnsen and Moe (in the 1840s) and Bjørnson (in the 1850s) had introduced a new colloquial style in their fairytale collections and peasant stories, respectively. Throughout the final decades of the nineteenth century, authors writing in Dano-Norwegian continued to develop the variety stylistically, using as their model the syntax and informal style of upper-middle-class speech (parallel to what Arne Garborg and others had done with Landsmaal).

In 1885, the Ministry of Church and Education cited the seventh edition of *Orthographic Rules for Use in Schools* (*Retskrivnings-regler til Skolebrug*) (Aars 1885) as the benchmark for how Dano-Norwegian words were to be written. This was the first time the Ministry officially authorised a specific model for Dano-Norwegian spelling. The later editions of the book served this purpose until 1907.

Towards the end of the nineteenth century, it finally became politically viable to argue for instituting changes to Dano-Norwegian in line with Knud Knudsen's programme. One of the greatest contributing factors to this was the political success of Landsmaal during the 1880s and 1890s. Hjalmar Falk (1859–1928), Professor of German at the University of Kristiania, claimed in a 1900 newspaper article that: 'In my opinion no reform [other than to Dano-Norwegian] is better suited to stealing the thunder from the advancing Landsmaal movement, whose most winning argument always will be the foreign-ness of the Dano-Norwegian standard' (Falk 1900, author's translation). By yielding on some points, they would, as Falk phrased it, 'steal the thunder' from the Landsmaal movement, and thus retain Dano-Norwegian's linguistic dominance. Many Dano-Norwegian users had begun to feel uneasy about the rapid progress of Landsmaal, and fear of a possible sociolinguistic revolution spread amongst them.

The fact that it took so long to agree on and implement changes to Dano-Norwegian was a clear drawback for its supporters. Preparations for reforming Dano-Norwegian were initiated in the early 1890s, starting in 1892 with the publication of the first edition of Nordahl Rolfsen's extremely important school reader. This book was subsequently used for nearly seventy years, and in its various editions was probably the country's most frequently read book after the Bible. In the first edition, Rolfsen included some word forms which were not authorised in Aars' *Orthographic Rules*, having been inspired and assisted by Moltke Moe (1859–1913), the son of fairytale collector Jørgen Moe and Professor of Folklore at the University of Kristiania. Moe was an enthusiastic supporter of reforming Dano-Norwegian according to Knudsen's principles (Andersen 1977: 173–83; Johnsen 2003: 406ff.). The unauthorised word forms he and Rolfsen introduced into the first edition came from upper-middle-class speech: for example *hester* (masc. pl. indef. 'horses', instead of Dan. *heste*) and *berg* (neut. pl. indef. 'mountains', instead of Dan. *bjerge*); past tense forms of some weak verbs, such as *strævde* and *talte* ('strove' and 'talked') instead of the Danish *strævede* and *talede*; plus *rope* (inf. 'call') and *blaase* (inf. 'blow') instead of the Danish *raabe* and *blæse*.

The following year, pupils were permitted to use all the new forms found in Rolfsen's reader in their school essays. This decision introduced a very important principle: that an individual could choose between different parallel word forms and morphological features. We shall see that this principle was exploited later on to a very large degree indeed in the various language reforms of the twentieth century. Before 1893, however, this was unheard of, and Aasen would never consider including such a principle in his standard. The notion of allowing parallel forms very soon became established as an obvious language planning tool and a useful means of introducing new forms alongside more traditional ones.

Quite soon, however, teachers reported that this new situation created difficulties for mother-tongue teaching because schoolchildren found it problematic to encounter forms in their reader that differed from those in all other texts. Even though they were allowed to use these upper-middle-class speech forms in their own writing, to most children they were as unfamiliar as the Danish forms had been.

This problem motivated the Ministry of Church and Education to embark on a total reform of Dano-Norwegian. Three experts were appointed to study the issue in 1897, and they submitted their report the next spring (Aars et al. 1898). The committee's recommendations were widely debated over the following years, and many people disagreed with the committee, which considerably slowed down progress on reforming Dano-Norwegian.

Only after the country put behind it the dissolution of the union with Sweden in 1905 did the groundwork for these changes resume. A meeting was called of eleven linguists, teachers and school headmasters in 1906 to discuss reform proposals. Two of the participants were asked to write new recommendations, which they completed the same autumn; this document was then scrutinised by three other experts, and the reform of the Dano-Norwegian standard was finally passed by the government in February 1907 (Nygaard 1945).

These reforms represented the final breakthrough for Knudsen's programme, since upper-middle-class speech was the exclusive basis for the changes, although many of these also had the effect of bringing the written forms closer to other spoken dialects. In many words, unvoiced stops (*p*, *t*, *k*) replaced the (Danish) voiced *b*, *d*, *g* in postvocalic position (for example *haap* < *haab* 'hope' n., *mat* < *mad* 'food', *bok* < *bog* 'book'). Shorter forms were introduced for a number of frequently used nouns and verbs, in accordance with upper-middle-class speech: *bror, far, mor* < (Danish) *broder, fader, moder* ('brother', 'father', 'mother'), *bli, dra, ha, si, ta* < (Danish) *blive, drage, have, sige, tage* ('become', 'leave/depart', 'have', 'say', 'take'). Plural forms of many common-gender nouns were reduced to the single endings *-er* (indef. pl.) and *-ene* (def. pl.) instead of the Danish system with two endings for each (indef. pl. *-er/-e* and def. pl. *-ene/-erne*): for example *hester* 'horses' (Dan. *heste*) – *hestene* (Dan. *hestene*) 'the horses'; *fester* (Dan. *fester*) 'parties' – *festene* (Dan. *festerne*) 'the parties'. The Danish past tense ending *-ede* for weak verbs was changed to three allomorphs (*-et*, *-te*, *-dde*) following the pattern in upper-middle-class speech for the 1st, 2nd and 3rd conjugations of weak verbs (for example *kastede* > *kastet* 'threw', *svarede* > *svarte* 'answered', *naaede* > *naadde* 'reached'). Adjectives ending in *-ig* would no longer add *-t* in the neuter form as in Danish (for example *et ærlig* (< *ærligt*) *menneske* 'an honest person').

Through the institution of these changes, the Dano-Norwegian standard (of Ibsen and Bjørnson) was transformed into Norwegian Riksmaal. The term 'Riksmaal' had been adopted by the Dano-Norwegian supporters in 1899, receiving a special endorsement from Bjørnson. It was almost immediately accepted as a suitable term for the Dano-Norwegian standard.

Norigs Maallag (1906), Riksmaalsforbundet (1907)

The two language movements now confronted each other like two armies preparing for war. Their debates were intense and often seemed to offer no compromise, and the tone was almost poisonous at times (cf. Hambro 1913). The Landsmaal movement united all its local associations in 1906 under a nationwide organisation called Norigs Maallag (Norway's Association for Landsmaal) (Hoel 2011: 47f.), and the Riksmaal movement responded in 1907 by creating Riksmaalsforbundet (The Riksmaal Association) (Langslet 1999).

They both proved to be very suitable and effective organisations in the language struggle (Almenningen et al. 1981).

Until 1907, the Norwegian language conflict was focused on Landsmaal versus Dano-Norwegian/Riksmaal – it was a clear-cut question of either/or. The Landsmaal movement was continuously on the offensive and achieved several important political victories between the 1870s and 1907. Starting from a mere suggestion by Ivar Aasen, Landsmaal had over the course of a few decades developed into a fully-fledged written standard that represented a real alternative, and threat, to the Dano-Norwegian standard. The political success of Aasen's programme was largely due to the fact that it became an integral part of opposition politics and the Liberal Party's programme. After the Liberals formed their first government, Landsmaal, as we have seen, received equal official standing with Dano-Norwegian in 1885.

In 1907, at long last, fundamental reforms to Dano-Norwegian resulted in its transformation into Norwegian Riksmaal, with all the changes based on upper-middle-class speech. The 1907 reforms represented the major break with the Danish language legacy in Norway, as from then on, even though many Landsmaal supporters continued to characterise Riksmaal as 'Danish', it was clear to most people that the subsequent language struggle was between two national – albeit sociolinguistically clearly different – standards.

The compulsory Landsmaal essay required for the high-school examination which was legislated for by Parliament in 1907 proved to be extremely provocative to large groups of Riksmaal users. They constantly characterised Landsmaal in degrading terms – calling it, for example, 'the cow barn language' (*fjøsmaal*) – which both disheartened and angered Landsmaal supporters. In 1910, Parliament rejected a proposal from Riksmaal supporters to revoke the 1907 decision. The candidates for high-school graduation came predominantly from social groups that harboured very little or no sympathy for Landsmaal, and many members of these groups felt that the decisions concerning exams constituted a warning that attempts would be made to introduce Landsmaal into all areas of society through legislation.

Each side in the language struggle was now prepared to attack the other party, and both aimed at inflicting total defeat on the other. Given the fact that such a high degree of tension existed only a few years after the break-up of the union in 1905, it is no surprise that a new, third voice emerged in the language conflict. Some people, frightened by the bitter tone of the debate and fearing that the newly won sense of national unity would be shattered, started searching for another alternative. Was there a possible language planning solution which did not involve one side losing? Could both sides win?

The one man in particular who emerged as the champion of this third way was Professor Moltke Moe (Moe 1909; Haaland 1980), the very person who in 1892 had been behind the introduction of unauthorised Dano-Norwegian word forms into Nordahl Rolfsen's school reader.

CHAPTER 5

Two Norwegian written standards: is linguistic reconciliation possible? Early twentieth century up to the 1917 language reforms

Political developments after 1905

In 1905, two referendums were held in Norway, one to approve Parliament's decision to dissolve the union between Norway and Sweden, and the other to determine whether the country would remain a kingdom or become a republic, with Prince Carl of Denmark being offered the throne. This second referendum was at the Prince's request; he would agree to become King of Norway if this was the will of the people. The result was a clear majority in favour of remaining a kingdom, and so Prince Carl of Denmark became King Haakon VII of Norway.

The union with Sweden between 1814 and 1905 had been symbolically important, signalling that Norway was not completely independent. However, its dissolution was quite insignificant in a political sense, since very few laws had to be changed in either country to accommodate the new situation. The main constitutional changes in Norway were simply that Norway now had its own king, as well as full control of its own foreign policy: the 1905 Government included a foreign minister for the first time in the country's history.

At the turn of the twentieth century, Norway was experiencing rapid industrial growth, basically due to the extensive exploitation of many of its waterfalls for hydroelectric power. This led to a substantial increase in the working-class population, as many people moved from the countryside to the towns and cities to find work, which in turn led to increased electoral support for the Labour Party. During World War I, economic and social questions increasingly moved to the political forefront. The times were difficult for a large portion of the population and there was serious social unrest, which led to even stronger support for the Labour Party.

After the introduction of parliamentary rule in 1884, governmental power had gone back and forth between the Liberal and Conservative parties. The language question had been one of the important issues on which they differed most. The Labour Party's main interest, however, was the economy; therefore, as its influence increased in every election after 1905, economic and social questions surfaced more frequently in political debates. Although the Labour Party was officially neutral regarding the language question, many of its leading members had a fundamental understanding of the social difference between Landsmaal and Riksmaal, and were quite often positive towards the Landsmaal cause (Hoel 2011: 289ff.), even though most of them used Riksmaal as their written standard.

During World War I, the Liberal Party enjoyed a solid majority in Parliament. However, after the 1918 election, it lost its absolute majority. This was the beginning of a long period of minority governments, most of which were in power for a relatively short period of time. During the 1920s, Conservative and Liberal Party governments lasted on average only about a year. The first Labour Government in 1928 was in power for only eighteen days. However, in 1935, Labour joined forces with the Peasants' Party and was thus able to form a government which had majority support in Parliament.

Nation building through great deeds and great authors

It was important for Norway as a young nation to prove itself and secure its place among the other Scandinavian and European nations. Several events and circumstances turned out to be especially important for boosting national pride towards the end of the nineteenth and beginning of the twentieth centuries.

The scientist Fridtjof Nansen (1861–1930), Nobel Peace Prize laureate for 1922, led several scientific and, indeed, daring expeditions to the Arctic between 1888 and 1896. He headed the first team to cross

Greenland on skis in 1888, and in 1893 he deliberately let his ship, *Fram*, be caught in the Arctic ice in order for it to drift across the Polar basin for three years. He and a companion headed out from the ship towards the North Pole in 1895, but were forced to turn back at the record northern latitude of 86 degrees and 14 minutes. When the ship finally returned to Norway, Nansen was received like a triumphal national hero. Together with Roald Amundsen's expedition to the South Pole in 1911, Nansen's achievements contributed immensely to fostering a sense of Norwegian national pride.

Adding considerably to their self-esteem was the fact that in the second half of the nineteenth century, Norway was clearly the leading Scandinavian country for literature, thanks to the works of a group of authors often referred to as 'the great four' (*de fire store*) – the playwright Henrik Ibsen, the Nobel Prize laureate Bjørnstjerne Bjørnson, and the novelists Alexander Kielland (1849–1906) and Jonas Lie (1833–1908) – who published most of their books in Copenhagen. The somewhat younger Knut Hamsun (1859–1952), Nobel Prize laureate for 1920, also contributed significantly to Norway's position as a country of great writers, as did Sigrid Undset (1882–1949), Nobel Prize laureate for 1928. All of these authors wrote their books in Dano-Norwegian/Riksmaal. At least three Landsmaal authors achieved the same level of quality in their writing: Arne Garborg, Olav Duun (1876–1939) and Tarjei Vesaas (1897–1970). Although all three were considered for the Nobel Prize on several occasions, none of them was ever awarded it.

Two national written standards

After the reforms to Dano-Norwegian in 1907, the nation faced a situation whereby it now had to accommodate two distinct and officially recognised written standards, both of which differed from the Swedish and Danish standards. Before then, it could be claimed that only one clearly Norwegian standard existed, that is, Landsmaal, since the other was only slightly different from the Danish written in Denmark.

Even though the orthographic reforms of 1862 represented a primary departure from Denmark's written standard – and minor changes had subsequently been implemented (for example, the abolition of capitalisation for nouns, officially from 1885, and of plural verb forms, officially from 1901, but implemented by most writers before

Figure 5.1   Henrik Ibsen (1828–1906), photo. (Source: Daniel Georg Nyblin/ National Library of Norway.)

that) – the Dano-Norwegian standard nevertheless appeared to most people to be quite similar to Danish. The 1907 reforms, however, were more fundamental and included changes to grammatical elements as well as to many frequently used individual words, which rendered Norwegian Riksmaal clearly distinct from Danish.

This fact is evidenced by the first known translation into Danish of a novel written in the 1907 Riksmaal standard, a crime novel published in 1913 (Jahr 1994: 45). When the book appeared in a second printing in 1919, it was published in two different editions, one for

Norway and one for Denmark; the latter was a Danish translation, a fact which, interestingly enough, was concealed from the readers and general public. The only difference between the two title pages was that the Norwegian edition stated it was published in 'Kristiania and Copenhagen', while the Danish edition gave the places of publication in reverse order. The publishing house obviously wanted to maintain the impression that the two countries still shared a common literary language, as they had done throughout the nineteenth century.

Early ideas about linguistic reconciliation

In view of the tone of the language conflict, it was no surprise when new reconciliatory solutions were proposed instead of complete victory for one side or the other. Professor Moltke Moe argued passionately and eloquently in favour of developing a pan-Norwegian (*Samnorsk*) written standard (Moe 1909), and he popularised the word *Samnorsk*, which had been used earlier by Arne Garborg (Hanto 1986: 114, note 11; Lomheim 2007: 296f.).

This idea of a pan-Norwegian standard obviously had strong appeal, as many people believed that the ongoing bitter language conflict was a major threat to national unity. Was the nation to be divided into two opposing language camps so soon after complete national independence had been won? It was one thing, however, to suggest that reconciliation, or a pan-Norwegian solution, had to be found, but quite a different one to develop a concrete method of achieving such a goal. Such a language planning programme, and subsequent policies to see it through, would need to be based on a sociolinguistic analysis of the whole language situation in Norway. In order to arrive at a realistic and feasible methodology for developing an amalgamated written standard, this analysis would need to include an understanding of the sociolinguistic characteristics of the two established standards; however, this was clearly lacking in the decade leading up to the 1917 language reforms.

The Eitrem Committee (1909) and minor reforms to Landsmaal (1910)

In 1909, a committee headed by a teacher, Hans Eitrem (1871–1937), published a report recommending changes to both Riksmaal and

Landsmaal that comprised the first steps in bringing the two standards closer together (Eitrem et al. 1909). However, since Riksmaal had undergone major changes only two years before, the authorities did not want to pursue the committee's suggestions for that standard. Many of the committee's recommendations were, however, followed up later in 1917.

In 1910, a minor and rather uncontroversial change to the Landsmaal standard represented the first concrete move in a pan-Norwegian direction. The changes introduced for certain noun endings followed some of the suggestions made by the Eitrem Committee and closed the linguistic distance with Riksmaal somewhat:

> weak fem. indef. sg. -a > -e: for example *visa* > *vise* 'song' (Riksmaal: *vise*)
> masc. def. pl. -arne > -ane: for example *stolarne* > *stolane* 'the chairs' (Riksmaal: *stolene*)
> strong fem. def. pl. -erne > -ene: for example *bygderne* > *bygdene* 'the parishes' (Riksmaal: *bygdene*).

These new forms had a rather restricted use as optional forms in schoolchildren's written essays. In 1917, however, these forms were all made obligatory in Landsmaal.

The 'Grimstad Affair' (1911–12): the first twentieth-century battle over dialect use in schools

In 1911, Knut Grimstad (1866–1924), a primary-school teacher from the town of Kristiansund on the western coast of Norway, refused to accept a directive by the town's school board to speak, and teach his pupils to speak, the Dano-Norwegian creoloid. Grimstad pointed to Parliament's 1878 resolution and refused to obey the directive. Although he was the only teacher in Kristiansund to openly dispute the school board's decision, Grimstad's individual protest was to have far-reaching consequences indeed (Jahr 1984: 150–289).

Gradually, this case grew into a heated debate in the newspapers, and the following year the 'Grimstad Affair' was put on the parliamentary agenda on various occasions. In the first part of 1912, articles about this issue were to be found on the front pages of the daily newspapers, competing with the *Titanic* tragedy as well as the race between

Roald Amundsen and Robert Scott to be the first explorer to reach the South Pole.

What was at stake here was the 1878 principle about dialect use in schools, or, rather, whether local school boards had been given the power in 1892 to disregard the 1878 resolution and select a spoken variety other than the local dialect for teaching purposes. The issue thus concerned the question of whether anybody – or any body – had the authority to choose upper-middle-class speech rather than the local dialect as the standard for oral instruction if Riksmaal was the written standard in that particular school.

The Kristiansund School Board had unanimously decided that spoken Riksmaal (the Dano-Norwegian creoloid) was to be used by both teachers and pupils during oral instruction. Their decision was eventually sent on appeal to the Ministry of Church and Education, which replied that the use of spoken Riksmaal was the logical consequence of that variety having been selected as the main written standard of the school. Upper-middle-class speech – the letter from the Ministry used the term 'Riksmaal' to refer to this variety – was therefore to be used by teachers and pupils during oral instruction. Mr Grimstad was criticised for opposing a perfectly legal decision. However, the issue of whether or not the board's decision was legal was not that easy to settle. Many people believed that the parliamentary resolution of 1878 was still valid, and that the Kristiansund decision was therefore in breach of this earlier decision.

During the 1878 debate in Parliament, several Members of Parliament – supporters of Landsmaal as well as others – had declared that the choice about which spoken variety should be used in schools was obvious, and that all wise teachers had long since practiced the principle upheld in the parliamentary resolution that the language of instruction in schools should be as close as possible to the pupils' dialect. Until 1892, when the language paragraph was included in the School Act of 1889 through an amendment, the only directive about language was that teaching was to be conducted in 'the Norwegian language' (*det norske sprog*). This formulation was open to many interpretations. While some people argued that it referred to the language in which the laws of Norway were written (that is, Danish, now interpreted as Riksmaal by most people), others claimed that the term 'Norwegian' implied a form of language which differed from Danish, meaning the Norwegian dialects and Ivar Aasen's Landsmaal.

The 1892 Language Paragraph Amendment to the School Act had empowered all the local school boards around the country to decide which of the two *written* standards was to be used by their pupils at school. But was the parliamentary resolution of 1878 on oral use still legally binding, or had the school boards been given the right in 1892 to choose the language of oral instruction as well? Many people claimed that the latter was the case. Although several Members of Parliament had stated during the 1892 debate that the change in the law was not intended to impinge on the regulation concerning spoken school language, their view on this matter was not to have any effect on what happened after the turn of the century.

Similar cases to the one in Kristiansund had arisen elsewhere – in Bergen and Trondheim in 1904 and in the small rural municipality of Eide in the southern coastal region of Agder in 1907. On both occasions the Ministry handed down the same decision: that a school board was entitled to determine which spoken variety would be used in school, including whether or not children were to receive instruction in the Dano-Norwegian creoloid (ibid.: 78–120, 131–43). So when the Grimstad Affair came onto the parliamentary agenda in 1911 and 1912, the Ministry of Church and Education had a firm basis in previous decisions for its claim that the Kristiansund School Board was fully entitled to insist that spoken Riksmaal was to be used in oral instruction instead of the local dialect. They argued that Grimstad's protest had no legal basis, in effect setting aside the parliamentary resolution of 1878.

The Kristiansund School Board reacted strongly against Mr Grimstad; however, he maintained that he had not intended to show disrespect to them, but had only wanted to draw attention to the fact that, in his view, they had taken an illegal decision. The conflict appeared to be about whether or not their decision was in keeping with the law. In reality, this whole affair was a battle between people who supported the use of local dialects in school and those who wanted to introduce spoken Riksmaal, that is, upper-middle-class speech, as a spoken standard. The importance of the Grimstad Affair had made it necessary to reach a political resolution, and so the point had been raised and discussed in Parliament.

This affair was very inconvenient for the government, which had promised to remain neutral on the language question. Landsmaal supporters across the country responded vehemently to the government's decision about the Grimstad Affair, and both Parliament and the Ministry of Church and Education received telegrams and letters protesting about 'torturing the tongue' of school pupils (ibid.: 216f.). The Education Minister, a former ardent supporter of Landsmaal, was fiercely attacked as a traitor to the Landsmaal cause.

Regulation of oral instruction through the School Act

The government soon realised that it had to act. There was an upcoming election in the autumn of 1912, and it did not wish to alienate the Landsmaal supporters, so it presented Parliament with a proposal to amend the School Act to incorporate the principle of the 1878 parliamentary resolution. But the government also had to take into account those who agreed with the Kristiansund School Board. The proposal therefore established that, in addition to instruction being given 'in the common spoken dialect of the place', oral instruction should ensure that the pupils were 'trained in the form of the language that had been chosen for their written work' in their Norwegian language classes. By drafting the passage in this way, the government hoped to please supporters of both Landsmaal and Riksmaal (ibid.: 237–43). However, Riksmaal supporters were very displeased, and the political reaction was fierce. The planned discussion of the proposal in Parliament was postponed – and in fact never occurred – because of the election.

This entire affair was in a political sense extremely unfortunate for the government and partly explains why the opposition Liberal Party won a landslide victory in the election. The new government withdrew the previous government's spoken language proposal, signalling that the 1878 resolution would be incorporated as it was into the School Act. The entire question of the spoken variety used in schools would thus finally find political resolution, with the defenders of local dialect use in schools having gained the upper hand.

In April 1914, the government proposed including the following language paragraph in the School Act; Parliament approved it in 1915 for rural schools and in 1917 for urban schools: 'For oral language, the pupils are to use their own spoken variety, and the teacher shall as far as possible adapt his natural spoken variety to the dialect of his pupils' (ibid.: 358; author's translation).

Changing views about urban dialects

In the meantime, a completely new motivation for the defence of local dialects, especially working-class urban dialects, had surfaced as a factor influencing the majority view in Parliament. This was the potential of these dialects for supplying linguistic material to develop, through careful language planning, a pan-Norwegian alternative as a solution to the intense rivalry between Riksmaal and Landsmaal.

This new attitude towards the dialects of the cities and towns contributed significantly to the changing language-political landscape between 1910 and 1920. The Landsmaal movement had originally paid little attention to urban dialects, viewing them as being too influenced by Danish and upper-middle-class speech to count as 'Norwegian', with little or nothing to contribute to the standardisation of the written language. This view coincided with the tenets of the Riksmaal supporters, who thought that urban dialects were nothing but vulgar and incorrect versions of upper-middle-class speech.

This change in attitude on the part of the Landsmaal movement was primarily brought about through the results of linguistic research. The leading Norwegian dialectologist of the time, Amund B. Larsen (1849–1928), published an in-depth monograph on the working-class dialect of Kristiania (Larsen 1907). His study convincingly showed that this urban dialect was closely related to the rural dialects surrounding the capital, and not to upper-middle-class speech. From the point of view of the history of linguistics, the early date of this study makes it a pioneering work in urban dialectology both nationally and internationally (Trudgill 1986: 69).

Østlandsk reisning (Eastern Norwegian Uprising) (1916–26)

During the decade 1910–20, urban dialects and those spoken in the central southeast of Norway came to play an increasingly important role in the language debate. These dialects were barely represented in Landsmaal, and Riksmaal had not shown any interest in them either. It was often mentioned that while Landsmaal had, for example, the form *soli* 'sun def.' and Riksmaal had *solen*, the southeastern dialects had *sola*; and *sola*, which was undoubtedly the form found in most Norwegian dialects around the country, was actually not permitted under any circumstances in either standard.

The demand for the eastern dialects to be given more prominence in language planning policies resulted in the establishment of the country's third language-political organisation, Eastern Norwegian Uprising (*Østlandsk reising*) in 1916. Its purpose was to ensure that the ignored southeastern dialects were taken into account in language planning decisions, and its leaders argued for the inclusion of features from these dialects in the written standards. The organisation operated between 1916 and 1926, and strove to encourage people in the eastern counties to use and be proud of their dialects (Jahr 1978).

From its very beginning, Eastern Norwegian Uprising defined itself as a pan-Norwegian organisation, and its leaders maintained that the dialects of the southeast had a historic role to play: they were able to furnish the written standards with sufficient linguistic material to bridge the division between the 'western-oriented' Landsmaal standard and 'urban-oriented' Riksmaal standard (ibid.).

Didrik Arup Seip (1884–1963), Professor of Riksmaal from 1916, was one of the leading figures in *Østlandsk reisning*, and argued that it would be possible to break the irreconcilable language policy deadlock between Landsmaal and Riksmaal, provided that the right choices were made. If the rural dialects of the southeastern counties – which were less archaic than the rural western dialects – were used to provide the basis for language reform, the result would be that the Landsmaal standard would be linguistically modernised and Riksmaal further Norwegianised. In this manner, the linguistic distance between the two standards could be decidedly reduced. Seip believed that this type of reform was later bound to move the language in a pan-Norwegian direction by virtue of its own momentum (Seip 1917; cf. Bleken 1966).

Many people shared Seip's and *Østlandsk reisning*'s views on this matter, but there were also many who disagreed and doubted that it was practically and politically possible to merge the written standards in this manner. It was clear that Seip's main arguments were based on the relatively trivial linguistic differences between the two standards. He did not fully realise that the sociolinguistic differences were far more important and would be very difficult to bridge in order to reach a planned, amalgamated pan-Norwegian standard which would be 'suitable for all Norwegians', according to one of Seip's slogans (Seip 1916b: 29).

The Torp Committee (1913)

After several years of deliberations over how to proceed with the two written standards – the Landsmaal 'Hægstad Standard' (*Hægstadnormalen*) after 1901 and Riksmaal after 1907 – several important opinion-makers took part in further discussions, among them Professor Fridtjof Nansen. Additionally, an internal committee of Riksmaalsforbundet submitted a report in 1913 (Riksmaalsforbundet 1913), but their recommendations were considered to be far too radical for most Riksmaal supporters, and therefore the report was not followed up. However, like the Eitrem Committee's 1909 report (Eitrem et al. 1909), this one contained recommendations for guiding Riksmaal away from its Danish origins, and it was to inspire many of the changes implemented later on in 1917.

While the internal Riksmaal committee was working on its report, the Ministry of Church and Education appointed an official committee in September 1913 whose mandate was to draw up plans for reforms to both standards. Their stated objective was 'national unity' (*national samling*), and their specific linguistic recommendations were to be based on 'the true spoken language of the people' (*folkets virkelige talesprog*). This was an extremely vague concept, wide open to various interpretations. The Ministry had originally suggested – in line with Knudsen's programme – that 'the educated spoken language' (*det dannede talesprog*, or upper-middle-class speech) should form the basis of changes, as it had in the 1907 reforms. Taking 'the language of the people' as a new normative base signalled the possibility of a totally different sociolinguistic direction for language planning policies.

Many years later, it was revealed in Parliament that the person behind this extremely important move away from basing language reforms on upper-middle-class speech was the history professor Halvdan Koht (1873–1965). Obviously, the vagueness of the wording which he persuaded the Ministry to include in the committee's instructions had been quite deliberate on Koht's part. Professor Koht was both a Landsmaal supporter and, from 1916, one of the leaders of *Østlandsk reisning*. In Chapter 6, we will learn more about his seminal role in the following decades, especially during the period between the two World Wars.

Linguistics professor Alf Torp (1853–1916) was appointed Head of the committee, which consisted of six members who were language experts or authors. They represented both the Riksmaal and Landsmaal movements, and they had a clear mandate to start working towards a pan-Norwegian alternative.

Breakthrough for a pan-Norwegian policy (1915–17)

Nobody at the time could imagine that the situation of having two national standards could continue, so a solution needed to be found which would lead to a single written standard. The desire to work towards linguistic unification was present in the preparation for the Torp Committee's mandate, but it took until 1915–17 for there to be a breakthrough for a pan-Norwegian policy among parliamentary representatives. Frequent debates on the question of which varieties should be used in oral instruction in schools, especially urban ones, played a very important role. Johan Gjøstein (1866–1935), a Labour Member of Parliament, argued vigorously during those years in favour of giving urban working-class dialects legally protected status in schools, because in his view they possessed the capacity to bridge the linguistic gap between Landsmaal and Riksmaal. On the other hand, *Østlandsk Reisning* argued that the southeastern rural dialects constituted the only linguistic basis on which to build a pan-Norwegian standard. What is important here, however, is not so much the difference between these two positions, but the fact that *spoken varieties other than upper-middle-class speech* were being postulated as possible resources for reconciling and ultimately merging written Landsmaal and Riksmaal into a pan-Norwegian standard. The southeastern and urban working-class dialects seemed to lend themselves to serving as links between the opposing camps.

A serious weakness in this analysis, which was not realised at the time, was the total lack of understanding and appreciation of the importance of the underlying sociolinguistic differences between the two written standards, as well as between upper-middle-class speech and the rural/urban popular dialects. The social distance was indeed far greater than the purely linguistic one.

The Falk Committee (1916)

The Torp Committee did not manage to proceed very far before they encountered serious disagreements amongst themselves. When

Alf Torp died in 1916, the Ministry of Church and Education set up a new committee, reducing the number of members from six to five. Only two of the original group were reappointed, and the new leader, Hjalmar Falk (1859–1927), Professor of German at the University of Kristiania, was a fresh face, as was Didrik Arup Seip, who had been made a professor earlier in 1916 at the age of thirty-two. Seip, as mentioned above, was one of the leaders of the new organisation *Østlandsk Reisning*, and had clear pan-Norwegian leanings. Seip took a very central role in the Falk Committee and probably wrote large parts of its final report. The document (*Indstilling* 1917), delivered on 12 December 1917, was therefore heavily influenced by his views.

Only nine days after the committee submitted its report to the Ministry, very close to Christmas 1917, the government accepted its recommendations and stated that future reforms to the two standards were to follow the proposals laid down in the report. This very rapid action by the government was heavily criticised later on, especially in 1918 when the general public became aware of it (Tryti 1953; Petersen 1977). Nobody outside the Ministry of Church and Education had seen the report before it was approved by the government, and so nobody had been able to voice an opinion either way about the committee's suggestions. In 1919, after the government had lost its absolute majority, it almost lost a crucial vote in Parliament about the 1917 language reforms. The government was saved, however, by the deciding vote of the parliamentary President, who happened to be from the Labour Party, signalling that Labour would play a more important role in the language struggle in the coming decades.

THE LANGUAGE REFORM OF 1917

The 1917 reform was the first serious attempt to work towards a pan-Norwegian standard; however, as such, it turned out to be rather unsuccessful. The resulting Riksmål and Landsmål standards were both split into two sub-varieties. (The letter *å* – for example, in these names – was introduced as optional for *aa* in 1917 and became obligatory in 1938.) One of the Riksmål sub-varieties was a close reflection of upper-middle-class speech, thus fulfilling Knudsen's programme from the nineteenth century. The alternative Riksmål sub-variety was considered by many people to be extremely radical, containing 'rude' and 'vulgar' linguistic forms, as it made frequent use of south-eastern popular dialect elements as well as forms which coincided with those of Landsmål. Thus, this version of Riksmål pointed in a pan-Norwegian direction – a direct result of changing the normative base from upper-middle-class speech to 'the true spoken language of the people', as laid down in the reform committee's mandates in 1913 and 1916.

Although Landsmål was also split into a more traditional, Aasen-like standard and a southeastern-based sub-variety, this had few consequences compared to the turmoil created by the two Riksmål varieties. However, it was clear that the more southeastern Landsmål sub-variety was the one which was moving in a clearly pan-Norwegian direction.

Confusing terminology

The 1917 reforms were accompanied by rather confusing terminology for the different word forms and sub-varieties of the two standards. The Falk Committee's report was to blame, though its intention was understandable and reasonable enough. The document started off by referring to changes in both standards which had to be universally accepted as 'obligatory changes'. The word forms affected by these changes were subsequently called 'obligatory forms' (*obligatoriske former*), since these were compulsory for everybody. The version of Riksmål which incorporated these changes (but only these) was then termed 'Riksmål with obligatory forms' (*riksmål med obligatoriske former*); similarly, there was 'Landsmål with obligatory forms' (*landsmål med obligatoriske former*). The final step saw the term 'obligatory' transferred to the actual sub-variety: Riksmål with only the compulsory changes (that is, with the minimum changes from the 1907 version) came to be called 'obligatory Riksmål' (*obligatorisk riksmål*), and the parallel standard was 'obligatory Landsmål' (*obligatorisk landsmål*).

However, the committee's mandate was also to recommend changes to both standards which would contribute to a pan-Norwegian development, that is yielding word forms and morphological features which pointed in a pan-Norwegian direction. The committee's suggestions along those lines were termed 'optional changes', meaning that people could use them according to their own wishes. This led to the concept of 'optional forms' (*valgfrie former*), and the resulting Riksmål sub-variety which went as far as possible along the pan-Norwegian path and accepted all possible changes was called 'Riksmål with optional forms' (*riksmål med valgfrie former*), and ultimately 'optional Riksmål' (*valgfritt riksmål*). The same held for Landsmål: 'Landsmål with optional forms' (*landsmål med valfrie former*), and finally 'optional Landsmål' (*valfritt landsmål*).

These names were obviously both misleading and confusing. Obligatory forms were not compulsory, since the optional forms were equally correct and usable. However, those who supported a Riksmål standard with as few changes as possible from the 1907 standard – free of all southeastern or working-class dialect elements – were quite pleased with the concept of 'obligatory Riksmål' as a name for the sub-standard they favoured. It was far more difficult to win support for a standard called 'optional Riksmål', the variety which pointed towards a pan-Norwegian solution and which incorporated the maximum number of southeastern and working-class dialect elements. These 'optional forms', and consequently 'optional Riksmål', were promoted by the organisation *Østlandsk reisning*.

Obviously, the Falk Committee had not intended that schools or individual writers would have to choose between a standard which incorporated either only the minimum or the maximum number of changes. Clearly they thought that various compromises would and should be made by individuals, and then after a limited period of use language planners could analyse where the standard was heading. Unfortunately, the committee led the authorities and others astray on this point, because in the final part of its report it presented its recommendations in the form of a single text rendered in the four different varieties: Riksmål and Landsmål with the minimum changes required, as well as with the maximum use of all the recommended changes taking them in a pan-Norwegian direction. It was not easy for readers to understand this presentation in any way other than as directing them to select one of the four new standards. This was the Ministry of Church and Education's interpretation, and school boards were therefore given the option of choosing either the more traditional or the more radical variety of either Riksmål or Landsmål.

Concrete changes to Riksmål

The orthographic principles that Aasen originally came up with for Landsmål were also applied to Riksmål, for example using double consonants after short vowels: *sett* < *set* 'seen', *gitt* < *git* 'given', *satt* < *sat* 'sat', with *nd/nn* and *ld/ll* distributed according to etymology: *mann* < *mand* 'man' (Landsmål: *mann*); *fjell* < *fjeld* 'mountain' (Landsmål: *fjell*); but *sand* 'sand' as before (Landsmål: *sand*), and *holde* 'hold' as before (Landsmål: *halda*). (Cf. *Den nye rettskrivning* 1917a.)

The feminine gender (found in Landsmål) was introduced into the radical (optional) sub-variety of Riksmål instead of the common gender used in upper-middle-class speech: *ei* or *e* for the fem. indef. article and postposed *-a* for the def. sg. article, for example:

ei/e sol – sola 'a sun' – 'the sun' (cf. 'obligatory Riksmål' *en sol – solen*) *ei/e flaske – flaska* 'a bottle' – 'the bottle' (cf. 'obligatory Riksmål' *en flaske – flasken*)

The radical, 'optional' variety of Riksmål also introduced the past tense and perfect participle ending *-a* for the 1st conjugation of weak verbs: *kastet* > *kasta* 'threw' (Landsmål: *kasta*), a feature not found in upper-middle-class speech, which instead had *-et*.

Diphthongs were allowed as options in many words, often rendering them identical to the Landsmål forms but deviating from upper-middle-class speech: *ben* > *bein* 'bone, leg' (Landsmål: *bein*), *løv* > *lauv* 'leaf' (Landsmål: *lauv*). In Riksmål with optional forms, many other frequently-used words were also altered from forms which reflected upper-middle-class speech to those which were identical with Landsmål:

frem > *fram* 'forward'
nu > *nå* 'now' (Landsmål: *no/nå*)
sprog > *språk* 'language'
syd > *sør* 'south'
efter > *etter* 'after'
sne > *snø* 'snow'
farve > *farge* 'colour'

However, in the more traditional Riksmål with obligatory forms, all these words remained unchanged; the common-gender system was also kept intact, with very few exceptions – some feminine nouns, mostly relating to rural life, were given feminine gender morphology, for example *furua* 'the pine tree', *kveita* 'the halibut', *kraaka* 'the crow', *kua* 'the cow', *rypa* 'the grouse' (ibid.: 19). Finally, in Riksmål with obligatory forms, the past tense ending for weak verbs of the 1st conjugation remained *-et*, which had been introduced in the 1907 reforms.

Concrete changes to Landsmål

The sub-variety that came to be called 'Landsmål with obligatory forms' was only slightly altered from the traditional (1901) standard but incorporated all the changes from 1910. The second, more radical variety, 'Landsmål with optional forms', included a large number of word forms and features from the southeastern dialects which drew it linguistically closer to the radical 'optional' Riksmål variety (*Den nye rettskrivning* 1917b).

One of the most important differences between the two standard Landsmål varieties concerned the declension of feminine nouns. While the more traditional variety kept Aasen's system of separate declensions for strong and weak feminine nouns, the radical variety did not distinguish between the two categories:

> 1901 Landsmål:
> strong fem.: *ei bygd – bygdi – bygder – bygderne*
>   'a parish' – 'the parish' – 'parishes' – 'the parishes'
> weak fem.:   *ei visa – visa – visor – visorne*
>   'a song' – 'the song' – 'songs' – 'the songs'

(The 1910 reform accepted *ei vise* (sg. indef.), *bygdene* and *visone* (pl. def.) in pupils' essays.)

> 1917 reforms:
> Landsmål with obligatory forms, that is, the traditional variety:
> *ei bygd – bygdi – bygder – bygdene*
> *ei visa – visa – visor – visone*

Landsmål with optional forms/Riksmål with optional forms:
ei/e bygd – bygda – bygder – bygdene
ei/e vise – visa – viser – visene

Riksmål with obligatory forms:
en bygd – bygden – bygder – bygdene
en vise – visen – viser – visene

In contemporary debates, the two Landsmål sub-varieties were often referred to as 'i-language' (*i-mål*, the variety with *bygdi* etc.), and 'a-language' (*a-mål*, with *bygda* etc.).

The 1917 reform of Riksmål as an omen of what to expect

In order to understand the struggle that followed the 1917 reforms, it is important to note that the two sub-varieties of Riksmål belonged on opposite sides of the most salient sociolinguistic divide in the Norwegian language community: between upper-middle-class speech on the one hand, and the combination of rural and urban dialects on the other. Linguistically and socially – the latter being the most important – the difference was less significant between 'optional Landsmål' and 'optional Riksmål' than it was between the two Riksmål sub-varieties. We may say therefore that the social dimension of the conflict between Riksmål and Landsmål that had been present before 1917 now existed even *within* official Riksmål, and that it found its expression in the two different sub-varieties of that standard.

The wording of comments by opponents of the 1917 reforms leaves little room for doubt that their reactions were based solely on a sociolinguistic and sociopolitical assessment of what had been done to Riksmål in this process. Nobody protested that the Riksmål standard had been 'Norwegianised' so that it was less marked by its Danish origin – which was given as the main motivation by the Falk Committee – but rather that their language had been 'vulgarised', 'raped' and 'Bolshevised'. These terms carry a clear social message: with the introduction of optional low-status words and grammatical elements into Riksmål, the class struggle – represented politically by the Labour Party and by an ever-growing working class – was infiltrating the written standard of the majority in the country. 'Riksmål with optional forms' reflected the language of different social classes from the more traditional variety's base. Opponents argued that 'culture' and 'education' were more under threat than ever before. To many members of the lower-middle class, language was often the main way of distinguishing themselves from the working class. Therefore, they could not accept the authorities' decision that something other than upper-middle-class speech forms would now be considered correct in the written standard. For them, upper-middle-class speech was characterised as being the 'correct' and 'nice' language, and using this variety was thus essential for them to retain their position in society (Tryti 1953: 184–8).

In parallel with 1917's Bolshevik Revolution in Russia, a sociolinguistic revolution 'from below' was threatening to engulf Norway, according to many of the protesters. This claim, however, was premature: the sociolinguistic revolution did not take place until 1938, as we will see.

The end of the nationalist period of language planning

The language reforms of 1917 represented the conclusion of the first Norwegian language planning period, which had focused on creating a national written standard. With the passage of these changes, it was obvious that *two* standards now existed, both of which could be called Norwegian since they were both based on spoken varieties which existed only within the geographic boundaries of Norway.

Within the nationalist framework, language planning had produced two competing written standards which were unquestionably quite different from both Danish and Swedish. The reforms of 1907 and 1917 had succeeded in changing written Danish by degrees into a Norwegian Riksmål standard. After 1917, the 'obligatory Riksmål' sub-variety reflected the spoken idiom of the upper-middle classes, which enjoyed by far the highest prestige in society at large, although it was not accepted as being truly Norwegian by large and influential groups of Landsmål supporters. In their view, only the total replacement of Riksmål with Landsmål would signify that the nation had succeeded in throwing off the colonial legacy of the long Dano-Norwegian union. This nationalist view had a strong appeal and led to further recruitment of supporters to the Landsmål cause. On the other hand, people who found it incorrect or even preposterous to suggest that upper-middle-class speech was not Norwegian for the most part opposed the Landsmål movement and rejected its goal of attaining total linguistic supremacy.

After the 1917 reforms, the language struggle changed quite dramatically. The main questions which surfaced during further language planning developments were of a sociolinguistic rather than nationalistic nature. In order to pursue the language planning policy of attaining a single, amalgamated written standard, the standards would need to move closer to one another through more language reforms. But because speakers of the upper-middle-class variety found their idiom reflected almost completely in one of the written Riksmål sub-standards after 1917, they saw no reason whatsoever to accept further alterations to it, nor could they accept the other variety of written Riksmål, which to them contained sociolinguistically unacceptable features. Thus, the nationalist ideology which had prevailed from 1814 to 1917 clearly provided an insufficient basis for developing a pan-Norwegian written standard, which by now had become the expressed goal of Parliament.

Within the nationalist framework, language planning up to 1917 must be judged as being very successful, having produced two unquestionably national written standards. However, the reaction of the upper-middle classes to the 'optional' word forms introduced into Riksmål in 1917 strongly indicated that language planning had reached the limit of what could be achieved within this framework. As long as changes to the Riksmål standard involved features found within upper-middle-class speech, they were reluctantly accepted, as was the case for the entire 1907 reform and the compulsory elements of the 1917 reforms. But when the language planners introduced features from the popular dialects into the Riksmål standard, they crossed the most important sociolinguistic boundary in Norwegian – the one between upper-middle-class speech and peasant- and working-class dialects.

After 1917, therefore, the language planning conflict took two distinct paths: the struggle within Riksmål, and the traditional struggle between Riksmål and Landsmål. The Landsmål movement only cared about the latter issue, but for the supporters of traditional Riksmål, the internal Riksmål battle soon became the dominant issue, and their struggle against Landsmål lost much of its intensity.

THE SOCIOPOLITICAL PERIOD, 1917–66

The emergence of a socialist theory of language planning: a sociolinguistic experiment

After the 1917 reforms, what was needed was a fresh analysis of the language situation on which to build a theory of language planning; and rather than focusing on what could be considered Norwegian versus Danish, it should concentrate instead on bridging the major sociolinguistic divide between popular local dialects and upper-middle-class speech. Doing this would involve defining the popular local dialects – understood as a single linguistic entity – as constituting the foundation on which not only Landsmål but also Riksmål should be based. It would also be necessary to identify the dialect forms that could be used to span the linguistic gap between the two standards.

In the aftermath of the 1917 reforms, there were once again heated debates in Parliament and in society at large about which spoken language varieties were to be used in schools. In addition, around the year 1930, Parliament decided to change the name of the city of Trondhjem to its medieval appellation, Nidaros (see further below). This triggered a fierce struggle both locally and nationally. In the end, the medieval name proposal was withdrawn and the change in spelling to Trondheim was agreed upon (Lockertsen 2007). These two conflicts convinced the Labour Party leaders that it was necessary to actively take steps to solve the language question once and for all (cf. Bernsen 1975; Rogne 1998).

The language political situation after the 1917 reforms

After 1917, then, the language conflict split into two fronts, making the situation considerably more complicated, with many people finding the contemporary state of affairs about language confusing and even intolerable. On the one hand, there was the continued competition between Riksmål and Landsmål: in the years immediately following the 1917 reforms, Landsmål gained considerable ground as the main standard in many school districts. On the other hand, there was now an internal struggle in the Riksmål movement between the more traditional variety and the new variety that was more radical in a sociolinguistic sense.

The political Riksmål movement, which grew considerably in numbers and strength in reaction to the 1917 reforms (Langslet 1999), concentrated its opposition on the use in schools of the sociolinguistically radical Riksmål variety. According to the leaders of this movement, this new variety, 'optional Riksmål', now represented a greater sociolinguistic threat than Landsmål did. The danger it represented could be compared to that of an indigenous guerrilla army, with Landsmål being more like an outside invader (Jahr 1980).

As far as schools were concerned, there was a fierce struggle in many local communities about which Riksmål variety to use. In many places, people experienced language-based conflict for the first time, especially in the southeast of the country, since competition between Riksmål and Landsmål had not yet reached this area. In many communities, the struggle turned out to be hard and bitter; indeed, in some places in the southeast, children were transported from one school district to a neighbouring one in order to avoid being forced to use 'optional Riksmål' as their language of written instruction. In the end, 64 per cent of the approximately 4,000 non-urban school districts nationwide where Riksmål was the principle standard decided to introduce 'optional Riksmål' (Jahr 1978: 153).

The organisation *Østlandsk reisning* had worked enthusiastically to spread the use of this variety in school. Two arguments were compelling for the municipal school boards when choosing the radical form of Riksmål. First, its morphology and word forms were, in general, closer to the spoken dialects of their pupils. Second, very few members of these school boards believed that the 1917 reform would be the final one, and 'optional Riksmål' seemed to indicate the direction in which the Riksmål standard was heading. From this perspective, 'obligatory Riksmål' appeared to be both conservative and backward-looking, even though in society at large it still dominated almost completely. Around 1925–6, this internal Riksmål struggle started to fade away as national economic problems became more pressing.

The newer 'optional Landsmål' standard also incorporated far more southeastern dialect forms, making it linguistically closer to the radical 'optional' Riksmål standard. However, this Landsmål sub-variety won very little support in the schools which had chosen Landsmål as their main standard, so on the whole there was less discussion within the Landsmål camp over the use of its two varieties.

The second struggle of the twentieth century over dialect use in schools – Bergen 1924

When the School Act was amended by Parliament in 1915 for rural schools, and 1917 for urban schools, the principle established in the 1878 parliamentary resolution became law; however, the conflict about dialect use in schools did not end with this new piece of legislation. It was one thing to have pupils' spoken language legally safeguarded, but it was quite another matter to ensure that this regulation was actually put into practice.

After some years, the country's seven School Directors were displeased to find that the regulations were not being respected in many schools. While this disobedience most frequently took place in urban schools, it certainly occurred in rural areas as well. In February 1923, the School Directors compelled the Ministry of Church and Education to issue a circular that explained and reinforced the content of the regulations – this caused a great deal of controversy.

That autumn, a majority of the Bergen School Board decided that both teachers and pupils in Bergen schools were to use spoken Riksmål in oral instruction since, they argued, spoken Riksmål was the local spoken dialect of its pupils. Their decision was brought to the attention of the Ministry by the local School Director. However, the issue was not dealt with until the following autumn. When the circular was issued in 1923, the sitting government was very positive towards Landsmål and the use of local dialects in general, particularly in schools. But when the matter was raised in Parliament in the autumn of 1924, a new and more conservative government was in power which was not as favourably disposed to these regulations.

In Parliament, the Minister was asked whether he and the Ministry of Church and Education considered the decision made by the Bergen School Board to be compatible with the regulations in the School Act. A long and intense debate on the issue followed over the next few days. In the end, Parliament agreed on the following statement, which was passed unanimously:

> Parliament asks the Ministry of Church and Education to ensure that the regulations in the School Act concerning the rights of pupils to employ their own spoken dialect in school and as far as possible to receive their instruction in this dialect be followed loyally and without any restrictions whatsoever or interventions on the part of the school authorities. (Jahr 1984: 443; author's translation.)

Shortly after this statement was released the government was defeated, and a more Landsmål-positive Liberal Party administration came into power. In 1925, the Ministry accordingly issued a new circular on the matter, stating that school boards did not have the authority to choose the spoken language used in school instruction. Decisions such as that taken by the Bergen School Board in 1924 would thus not be binding on teachers or pupils (ibid.: 447–50).

The events of 1924 represented the last serious conflict over the issue of the spoken language used in schools. Since then, most people have accepted the ruling that pupils are entitled to use their own local dialects in school, and that teachers should encourage them rather than correct them when they do so. Over the years, this principle has effectively prevented any spoken variety of Norwegian from being defined as the standard and taught in schools.

Bokmål and Nynorsk (1929)

In 1929, when Parliament was discussing an amendment concerning teacher training colleges, it voted to adopt what are now the current names of the two written standards: *Bokmål* (instead of Riksmål) and *Nynorsk* (instead of Landsmål). In 1914, some Landsmaal supporters in Parliament had acted quite provocatively by suggesting changing the names to 'Norwegian' (*norsk*) for Landsmaal and 'Dano-Norwegian' (*dansk-norsk*) for Riksmaal. This earlier proposal was met with disgust by Riksmål supporters, both in Parliament and among the general public, and it was not taken seriously (ibid.: 130, note 1). However, in 1929, the terms Bokmål ('book language') and Nynorsk ('new Norwegian') were agreed without a great deal of controversy. (We will use these names when discussing developments from 1930 onwards.)

The Labour Party gets involved. Halvdan Koht's analysis: 'the people's language'

Ever since Norwegian political parties emerged in the 1880s, the liberal *Venstre* ('Left') party in principle favoured Landsmaal (Haugland 1974), while the conservative *Høire* ('Right') party supported the Riksmaal cause (Lind 1975). However, Venstre's members did not unequivocally back the Landsmaal movement. The party experienced many internal conflicts which ended with groups of supporters leaving, to form new political groups or parties, or to join the other two established parties, Høire and Labour. Moreover, after 1906, Høire had to consider the views of their members who lived in the western counties in which the Landsmaal cause was important. The Labour Party, which grew stronger and more influential with each succeeding election, officially remained neutral on the language question and allowed its representatives to vote according to their own opinions.

When the 1917 reforms were implemented, school boards had to choose between the two sub-varieties of either Landsmål or Riksmål. In the case of rural Riksmål schools, this proved, as we have seen, to be the start of a battle between the more traditional and more radical Riksmål varieties. Here, often for the first time, the Labour representatives had to choose between, on the one hand, the variety which incorporated word forms and morphological features taken from local and working-class dialects and, on the other hand, the variety which mirrored upper-middle-class speech.

For many Labour representatives this proved to be quite an eye-opener. When they heard supporters of the more traditional Riksmål variety use words like 'vulgar', 'uneducated', 'ugly', and so on, about working-class dialects and forms, many of them decided they had to become actively involved in the language struggle. Before the 1917 reforms, the competition had only been between Landsmål and Riksmål, so many of them had not seen the relevance of the issue for urban working-class people. Now, however, the Riksmål standard consisted of two sociolinguistically very significantly different varieties – one associated with the working class, and one which was tied to the upper-middle classes, albeit a bit more problematically, since the latter also represented the older written tradition. This meant that it was now easier for Labour Party representatives to see the direct relevance of the language struggle for their urban working-class constituents.

Thus, the 1920s saw developments within the Labour Party which, however, did not have any direct effect on the party's official language policy until the end of the decade. Professor Halvdan Koht, a Labour Party member since 1911, was asked by the party leaders in 1920 to carry out an analysis of the language issue, and his report was meant to serve as the basis for hammering out the party's language planning programme (Søilen 1978). Nowhere in the theoretical works of leading international socialist figures such as Marx, Engels, Lenin and Eduard Bernstein could one find an analysis of language that would guide the Labour Party towards a language planning policy which would be appropriate for a Norwegian socialist party. And nobody at the time viewed a two-standard situation as viable for the future. The only possible solution for a small and poor country like Norway had to be a single standard. The party leaders hoped that Koht could point them in the right direction.

Koht's report appeared in 1921 as a small booklet in which he presented an analysis of the language situation, and the connection between language and social class, as being an integral part of Norwegian history. Koht outlined a language planning programme in which it was absolutely necessary to bridge the major sociolinguistic gap between the popular dialects of the common people and upper-middle-class speech. This implied assigning to the popular dialects the role of the linguistic foundation on which both Riksmål and Landsmål were to be developed. Koht's view was that the nineteenth-century rise of the peasants had to be continued in the twentieth century for both peasants and the urban working class. At the time, the Liberal Party was in the process of losing its former leading position as the champion of a democratic peasants' movement; and it was the Labour

Party which now installed itself as the political expression of the rise of the lower classes.

Koht viewed standard Landsmål as being too archaic and remote from contemporary working-class speech, and standard Riksmål as being too dependent on upper-middle-class speech, and also on written Danish even after the reforms in 1907 and 1917. Modernising Landsmål linguistically and, at the same time – and with the same linguistic tools – making Riksmål more democratic and national, would grant higher social status to what Koht called 'the people's language' (folkemålet).

A sociolinguistic understanding of the situation was fundamental to Koht's analysis. He argued that the only solution to the language issue was a sociopolitical one in which the lower classes – workers and peasants – co-opted both of the written standards by simultaneously introducing into both of them increasing amounts of current popular speech (reflecting phonology, morphology and lexis). The two standards would thus, by degrees, move closer together, and the process would lead to a devaluation of the upper-middle-class spoken variety. This demotion of upper-middle-class speech was absolutely necessary in order for an amalgamated written standard incorporating low-status forms to emerge and gain the necessary social prestige.

Koht's conclusion was that the Labour Party should include in its political programme a passage supporting a language planning policy that would promote 'the people's language' in both the Landsmål and Riksmål standards. As he put it at the very end of his analysis: 'The struggle to advance the people's language is the cultural side of the rise of the workers' (Koht 1921: 22; author's translation). Despite Professor Koht's recommendations, the Labour Party's internal processes meant that progress on this issue was very slow during the 1920s (Jahr 1976a). Apparently, nothing much happened until the fierce battle broke out in Trondhjem towards the end of the decade over changing the city's name.

The Norwegianisation of place names

The suggested change of name for Trondhjem was part of a larger process whereby place names throughout the country were given new forms and spellings. During the centuries of union with Denmark until 1814, all place names in Norway were spelled according to

Danish orthographic principles. As awareness of this Danish legacy grew after 1814, an extensive process began, aimed at 'reclaiming' place names from Danish by Norwegianising them. This was a huge and almost overwhelming undertaking which took several decades to complete. In some places, people protested vociferously against the changes, as they had grown accustomed to the Danish forms; however, most often the new names were reluctantly accepted.

Many of the protests were motivated by the fact that the underlying norm for this process of Norwegianisation was the orthographic system laid down by Ivar Aasen for Landsmål. This was an obvious choice, since Riksmål followed Danish orthographic principles to a large extent until the 1917 reforms. In areas of the country where Landsmål had not gained a strong foothold, especially in the southeast, place names that sounded very 'Landsmål' were not readily accepted by the general public.

One example comes from just outside the capital. The written form of the village's name was *Kullebunden* (meaning 'coal-bottom [of a valley, fjord etc.]') until 1920, when it was changed to *Kolbotn*, the Landsmål form. The local dialect pronunciation, however, would have been better rendered as *Kølabonn* (Vinje 1978: 335, note 2). The name change stirred up a great deal of debate and anger in the local community. Over the course of time, however, the inhabitants of the municipality grew accustomed to it, and today very few residents are aware of the older version of the name.

The Norwegianisation of place names encompassed cities and towns as well as smaller locations. The name of the capital itself was changed from Kristiania to Oslo on 1 January 1925, without much fuss (Wetås 2000). But when in 1929 Parliament decided to change Trondhjem to Nidaros, the city's medieval name (Lockertsen 2007), the townspeople mobilised to protest, demanding that it be changed back. After two years of intense conflict and political turmoil of proportions unseen in the language struggle up to then, a compromise was reached. Halvdan Koht, among others, suggested the name Trondheim, with the suffix *-heim* 'home' spelt the Landsmål/Nynorsk way. The suffix *-hjem* was used in Riksmål/Bokmål (and Danish), but since it was also common in dialects covering large areas of the country many people claimed that *-hjem* was a perfectly acceptable Norwegian linguistic form (Seip 1930). In Landsmål/Nynorsk, *-heim* was the only accepted form, and this won out.

The Labour Party finally adopts a language planning policy

In September 1929, more or less as a direct reaction to the turmoil in Trondheim, Labour Party leaders appointed an internal committee of five prominent members to draw up a language and cultural policy for the party. It now appeared obvious to the Labour leaders that a party that aspired to govern the country, as they did, not only had to hold a coherent view on the current language situation but also have a vision and policy about how to solve the language problem. Professor Koht was once again called upon and was appointed Chairman of the committee. As mentioned earlier, Koht had already offered an analysis of, and the historical background to, the language issue in his 1921 booklet, but discussion within the party had not led anywhere. The leaders felt that it was now high time for such deliberations, and the feud over Trondhjem's name made it apparent to everyone else that the time was ripe.

Before the Labour Party's general convention in March 1930, the Koht Committee issued a short statement declaring, among other things, that the party would always fight for 'the genuine people's language' (*ekte folkemål*), understood as the spoken varieties of the peasants and working-class people. The party would promote the use of 'all living people's language' in 'the press and the school'. The committee stated that the ultimate goal was that the two official written standards would 'in the end' be merged into a single standard reflecting the everyday speech of both peasants and the proletariat (Rykkja 1978).

At the 1930 convention, Koht delivered a comprehensive talk in which he outlined his analysis of the contemporary sociolinguistic situation. He argued that culture and language must always be viewed within a framework of class conflict. The upper classes would always refer to their culture and language, both spoken and written, as the only proper and worthwhile version, and to the speech and dialects of the lower classes as 'vulgar'. This was a general situation found in all modern societies, according to Koht. However, in Norway, the circumstances were somewhat different. Here, it was more apparent than in other countries that a national language policy was interwoven with the general class perspective. In promoting a 'Norwegian' stand-ard over a 'Danish' one, it was clearly the case that the lower classes represented the former while the upper-middle classes represented

Figure 6.1   Halvdan Koht (1873–1965), photo. (Source: Ivan Benkow/National Library of Norway.)

the latter. Thus, Koht argued, the combination of a nationalist and class-based language policy could work in Norway. The sociolinguistic concept which in Koht's view summarised the common interest of the peasants and the proletariat was 'the people's language'. Thus he concluded that the Labour Party should not support either Bokmål or Nynorsk, but instead promote the incorporation of 'the people's language' into both standards. In due time, this would lead to a merger of the two standards into a single pan-Norwegian standard, thus solving the language problem (Det Norske Arbeiderparti 1933).

After Koht's presentation there was no discussion. The convention unanimously adopted a statement that had been prepared by the party leaders beforehand asking the Koht Committee and the Labour Party Board to carry out further work based on the reports the committee had already submitted (Rykkja 1978: 175f.). This was somewhat surprising given that the experience from the Trondhjem-Nidaros controversy indicated the need for immediate and stronger involvement by the Labour Party. However, their general policy at the 1930 convention focused on being a party exclusively for the working class. Koht's emphasis on national cooperation between the peasants and the proletariat, symbolised by the concept of 'the people's language', was not yet in keeping with general party policy.

In the national elections in the autumn of 1930, the Labour Party lost several parliamentary seats, a major setback which was interpreted by many as a direct result of their very radical political decision to stay on as a party representing only the interests of the working class. At the same time, the impact of the world economic crisis hit the country hard. In 1931, unemployment among trade union members was between 30 per cent and 40 per cent. In the countryside, the crisis was devastating for many peasants, especially those with small farms (cf. Kjeldstadli 1994).

This situation led to a major change of course for the Labour Party. At its general convention in May 1933, it changed direction from being a declared revolutionary and socialist party to becoming a more classically European social-democratic party. The new party policy stated that a socialist society – their ultimate goal – could be attained not necessarily through a socialist revolution but through state capitalism.

This change of course gave Koht's language programme, based on the varieties of the urban and rural lower classes combined, an opportunity to come to the fore in party policy. Before the 1933 convention, a booklet entitled *Language and Other Cultural Questions* (*Sprog og andre kulturspørsmål*) was distributed within the party, containing all the material that had been presented at the 1930 convention: Koht's lecture, the statement from the party's Language and Culture Committee (the Koht Committee), as well as the text of the decision to continue working towards a Labour Party policy on these issues. However, no decision was taken on this at the 1933 convention either, and in fact the language question was not even on the agenda. Nonetheless, it was apparent that Koht's analysis and language programme now fitted the party's general political policy and strategy perfectly (Søilen 1978). The time was right for Koht's recommendations, and it seems likely that the party leaders took this more or less for granted and considered it unnecessary to present them as a special item to be voted on by the convention delegates.

It had long been Koht's objective for the peasants and the proletariat to join forces politically (Jahr 1976b; Søilen 1978; Bucken-Knapp 2003: 68f.). It was not all that easy for everybody within the party to appreciate the common political interests of these social classes; however, this had now been decided as the official party line. To Koht, the dialects of the peasants and the urban working class, defined as 'the people's language', were the most salient features binding the two social groups together. Therefore, working to promote 'the people's language' was not only a goal in its own right, but was also an important means of demonstrating and fostering cooperation and political unity between the combined lower classes against the upper-middle classes. In 1933, the Labour Party fully embraced this policy and promoted this message through a very effective election slogan: '*By og land, hand i hand!*' ('Town [= the urban working class] and countryside [= the peasants], hand in hand'). The alliance was even signalled through the form of the word *hand*, which was common to both the rural and urban working-class dialects, as opposed to the spoken upper-middle-class form *hånd* which does not rhyme with *land*. Thus, this slogan demonstrated Koht's programme and policy in a nutshell: language unites the lower classes and demonstrates that they have a common political interest against the upper-middle classes.

The Labour Party won a landslide victory in the election, taking over 40 per cent of the votes and nearly doubling its number of seats in Parliament. Combined with the Peasants' Party they held a clear majority. Labour formed a government in 1935, supported in Parliament by the Peasants' Party. Koht was appointed Foreign Minister, a post he held till he resigned in 1942 in London, where the Norwegian King and Government sat in exile during the Nazi occupation (Svendsen 2013).

Parliament appoints a new Language Commission (1934)

In the summer of 1933, Labour representatives in Parliament initiated a debate about further language reforms. They suggested that an official language commission be appointed with a mandate to continue planning a pan-Norwegian standard based on 'the people's language'. This was the first time Labour had taken such a step, and it indicates that by now Koht's programme had been fully adopted by the party. In May 1934, Parliament, with support from Labour, the Liberal Party and the Peasants' Party, passed the mandate for a new Language Commission which would have dual objectives: (1) to bring the two written standards linguistically closer to each other by introducing changes based on 'the people's language', and (2) at the same time, to cut down on the large number of optional forms allowed in both standards as a result of the 1917 reforms.

The three parties thus agreed to work towards a unification of the two standards by dramatically broadening the sociolinguistic basis of Bokmål. This time, popular dialect formulations would not just be given the status of optional parallel forms, as in 1917, but to a large degree they would become the main or only standard forms, thus considerably diminishing the influence of the most prestigious spoken variety in the country on standard written Bokmål. Parliament had indeed laid the foundations for a possible sociolinguistic revolution in Norway.

Clearly, this mandate was not an easy one to fulfil. In 1917, the new sociolinguistically more radical forms had been introduced as optional in order to make the changes more acceptable, placing the older and newer forms in a sort of competition. However, this method could also be interpreted as merely the first step in a process; the next step would be to make the new forms compulsory. This seemed to be the Ministry's plan, as can be seen in its instructions to the Language Commission before it started its deliberations:

> Word forms and inflections which have a broad popular
> base (majority forms) should be adopted as sole forms in
> both languages in so far as they harmonize with the inner
> organization and structure of each, and where considerations of
> tradition do not offer too great an obstacle. Danish forms and
> minority forms are to be abolished correspondingly. (Quoted
> from Haugen 1966a: 121.)

Undoubtedly, the phrase 'Danish forms and minority forms' meant upper-middle-class speech forms, which were to be abolished and replaced by those which had 'a broad popular base' – in other words, taken from 'the people's language'.

Interestingly enough, only one linguist was appointed to the Language Commission – Professor Ragnvald Iversen (1882–1960), who was an expert on historical linguistics as well as dialectology and who represented the Bokmål side, was made the Chairman. The other two Bokmål representatives were the author Johan Bojer (1872–1959) and the Labour politician and former schoolteacher Gustav Natvig-Pedersen (1893–1965), a Member of Parliament from 1937. The Nynorsk section was headed by Professor Halvdan Koht and included another historian, Arne Bergsgård (1886–1954), and a school principal, Martin Birkeland (1884–1954). None of these six was from the capital, Oslo, or even from southeastern Norway. While this fact was later heavily criticised, it was clearly a deliberate choice and indicates that the political authorities regarded this particular composition of the Language Commission as the best way to ensure that it would embrace the language planning policy delineated by Parliament's mandate.

Koht was without question an extremely influential member of the Commission. He was probably the most dedicated of the six in ensuring that their recommendations were in accordance with the mandate. The mandate itself was completely consistent with the pan-Norwegian language planning solution that Koht had argued for over the past twenty years, and which was now the official policy of the Labour Party. During the working life of the Commission Koht became Foreign Minister, but this in no way reduced his influence in the Language Commission. On the contrary, most of the report's recommendations bear his mark and must have been endorsed by him.

The Commission's first report (*Tilråding* 1935) clearly showed that the dual mandate had proved to be difficult. Reducing the numerous parallel forms was problematic, and it turned out to be impossible to agree fully on which widespread popular forms to promote and which minority forms to abolish. The Commission devised a way around this by introducing an entirely new hierarchical system of parallel linguistic elements within the standards: 'main' forms with higher status and 'minor' forms with lower status. In 1917, 'obligatory' and 'optional' forms had equal formal status within the standards; the test of this was that both were allowed in school textbooks. The Language Commission's new system distinguished between main forms (Bokmål *hovedformer*, Nynorsk *hovudformer*) which were allowed in school textbooks, and minor forms (*sideformer*) which were not. The minor forms were to be allowed in pupils' written essays; however, after 1938 these would appear on word lists and in dictionaries within square brackets [ ], so they were commonly referred to as 'bracket forms' (*klammeformer*).

The Commission's report was debated and publicly criticised by both the more conservative Nynorsk camp and the supporters of the traditional Riksmål variety. The Commission then issued an additional report in response to these criticisms. In June 1937 the new package of reforms was debated in Parliament over the course of an entire day, with as many as thirty-two members of Parliament speaking on the topic, some of them more than once. It was passed by one hundred and twelve votes to thirty-seven. Koht, now a member of the government, used the opportunity to drive home his language planning programme. He underlined once more the common interest, as he saw it, between the peasants and the proletariat, the very foundation of his political language planning programme:

> The restoration of Norwegian started with the rise of the peasants, and its natural continuation was the rise of the workers . . . It is the great goal of the Labour movement to crush class boundaries, to establish a national people's culture, and therefore it is natural that the working class now joins the peasants' movement in support of the language programme which leads to complete national unification. (*Stortingstidende* 1937: 1757; author's translation.)

The parliamentary opposition suggested that the reform be postponed and reviewed once more. The new Labour Minister of Church and Education promised that a review committee would be asked to go through all the recommendations made by the Language Commission. A three-member committee was appointed, all regarded as experts on Norwegian, whose opinions, however, soon proved to be divided on many of the debated issues. Their report was submitted in December 1937; the reforms were finally approved and passed by the government in January 1938, and put into effect on 1 July 1938 (Kirke- og undervisningsdepartementet 1938).

We have followed the developments from 1933 up to when this reform was formally adopted in 1938 in order to show how political this language planning process really was, and how interwoven politics was in its entire fabric. After the 1917 reforms, many people were very upset by what they considered to be a 'language coup'. This time, however, the package of reforms had been initiated and discussed in Parliament and in public for several years, and it had been drafted by both the Language Commission and the expert committee before finally being passed by the government. Even though many people viewed the reforms as representing the complete destruction of their language – and they said so (cf. Øverland 1940) – no one could claim that the process had not been thorough this time. The Labour Government was able to guide language planning in the direction laid down in its party's policies. Through a long, internal political process, Koht's analyses and views had finally been adopted.

The 1938 reforms in Bokmål and Nynorsk

Perhaps the most important systematic feature introduced into Bokmål in the 1938 reforms was the obligatory use of the feminine definite article -a for around 900 feminine, mainly concrete, nouns: for example, *boka* 'the book', *dokka* 'the doll', *flaska* 'the bottle', *høna* 'the hen', *jenta* 'the girl', *sola* 'the sun'. The traditional definite ending was masculine/common gender -*en*, which was most frequently found in upper-middle-class speech. For a number of feminine, typically abstract nouns, but also others, the definite ending -*a* was not made obligatory, so the choice was between -*a* and -*en*: for example, *tid-a/-en* 'the time', *makt-a/-en* 'the power', *sjel-a/en* 'the soul', *jul-a/en* '(the) Christmas', *tung-a/-en* 'the tongue', *jakt-a/-en* 'the hunt', *kvinn-a/-en* 'the woman', *uk-a/-en* 'the week'.

Incorporating the feminine definite singular ending -*a* into Bokmål was seen as extremely important for the evolution of a future pan-Norwegian standard. Therefore, this was also established as the main ending in Nynorsk for all feminine nouns. This change went against Aasen's system, which differentiated between strong and weak feminine nouns, ending in -*i* and -*a* respectively. This dual-ending system was still accepted in Nynorsk after 1938, but only as a 'minor' form, which meant that it could not appear in textbooks.

Another very important morphological feature which would bring the two standards closer together was use of the past tense ending -*a* for weak verbs of the 1st conjugation. In Nynorsk, it had been obligatory for this verb conjugation since 1901 (while the Aasen Standard had -*ade*). The Danish ending -*ede* had been superseded in Riksmaal in 1907 by -*et*, from upper-middle-class speech. In 1917, the -*a* ending, which was used in most popular dialects throughout the country, was introduced into Riksmål as an optional form, but this had not caught on to any great extent in writing (Pettersen 1993). In 1938, again -*a* was not made compulsory in Bokmål for more than a few verbs, even though this was considered absolutely necessary for a pan-Norwegian standard to emerge and succeed. So, after 1938, the use of the past tense ending -*et* continued unabated in Bokmål.

Therefore, since the use of the -*a* ending for past-tense weak verbs was not made mandatory in 1938 but only given equal formal status with the traditional -*et* ending, this was a clear indication that the 1938 reforms too, however sociolinguistically radical they might be, were only meant as additional steps – and not the final ones – in the direction of a future pan-Norwegian solution. New reforms obviously had to follow in order to achieve a pan-Norwegian single-standard situation.

For individual words where the upper-middle-class spoken form differed from most of the popular dialects, the version defined as coming from 'the people's language' was now often made obligatory in Bokmål. This meant that the upper-middle-class spoken forms either were made optional, or were deemed to be 'minor' forms, or were eliminated from the Bokmål standard altogether. In most cases this constituted quite a dramatic shift from the traditional standard. In 1917, the dialect-based forms had in many cases been made optional, but they tended not to be used very frequently in Bokmål. After the 1938 reforms, most of these words were the same in Bokmål and Nynorsk. All the older forms listed below, that is those used in upper-middle-class speech, were removed from the Bokmål standard; some of them coming to acquire a symbolic value for the Riksmål movement during in the 1950s:

efter > *etter* 'after'
frem > *fram* 'forward'
hård > *hard* 'hard'
mave > *mage* 'stomach'
nu > *nå* 'now'
sne > *snø* 'snow'
sprog > *språk* 'language'

Many other word forms which differed from the upper-middle-class spoken versions were also made obligatory, for example: *lauv* 'leaf', *reir* 'nest', *bru* 'bridge', *røyk* 'smoke', *kald* 'cold', *sju* 'seven', *tjue* 'twenty', and many more (the upper-middle-class speech forms were: *løv, rede, bro, røk, kold, syv, tyve*). Other words, such as *dokke* 'doll', *gras* 'grass', *rein* 'clean', *sein* 'late', and many more, were made the 'main' forms and thus were obligatory for school textbooks, while the upper-middle-class (and Riksmål) spoken forms – *dukke, gress, ren, sen* – were reduced in the Bokmål standard to 'minor' forms ('bracket forms').

The infinitive ending for verbs was also altered. This change affected Nynorsk more than Bokmål. Before 1917, Landsmål used only the ending *-a* in the infinitive, the form found in many of the western dialects. Many other dialects, however, including upper-middle-class speech, had *-e* as the infinitive ending, as in Riksmål/Bokmål. In 1917, the *-e* infinitive was introduced as optional in Landsmål. In addition to the alternative endings *-a* and *-e*, local dialects over large areas of the southeast – the most densely populated region of the country – featured a very special dual/'cleft' infinitive system with the *-a* ending used for some verbs and the *-e* ending for others, depending on the prosodic pattern of the verb in medieval Old Norse. For example, *lesa* 'read', *sova* 'sleep', *vera* 'be', *eta* 'eat', *komma* 'come' had the *-a* ending, while, for example, *skrive* 'write', *kaste* 'throw', *klatre* 'climb', *bygge* 'build', *løpe* 'run' had the *-e* ending. In 1938, the *-e* ending and the dual system were made parallel 'main' forms in Nynorsk, that is they were given equal status, while the older *-a* ending, from the Aasen Standard, was demoted to 'minor' status. For Bokmål, the *-e* infinitive continued as the 'main' form, but with the dual infinitive as a 'minor' form. Some people obviously thought that the dual infinitive could serve as the infinitive ending in both Bokmål and Nynorsk, since the dialects that had this feature represented a small majority of the country's total population. However, the difficulty in learning which verbs took which ending for people who did not have it in their native dialect ought to have convinced everyone that the dual infinitive would not win out in a future pan-Norwegian standard. (On the status and use of the dual/'cleft' infinitive in the two standards see Jahr 2010.)

What we observe here is a mixture of various motivations for choosing one linguistic form over another with regard to both Bokmål and Nynorsk. The norm on which the entire 1938 reform was based was 'the people's language', but when it failed to yield one obvious single solution, posing instead several possibilities, other reasons surfaced for making choices. For example, population counts were used to discover which linguistic forms had the most users in the dialects of the various geographical areas.

Aasen had already cited aesthetic reasons for some of the choices in his standard, for example for using a variety of different vowels or endings to create a more euphonic effect. In the 1938 reforms, this motive of aesthetic compensation resulted in the introduction of the -*i* ending for the past participle of strong verbs (instead of -*e*) in Nynorsk to compensate for the loss of -*i* as the main ending for the definite singular of feminine strong nouns (and the definite plural of most neuter nouns). There was a solid basis in the popular dialects for choosing the past participial strong verb ending -*i*: dialects covering large areas of the country, especially the southeast, used it; for example *eti* 'eaten', *komi* 'come', *skrivi* 'written'. The fact that any further reform of Bokmål in the direction of a pan-Norwegian standard would need to adopt the -*i* ending (instead of -*et*) for strong verbs probably also played a part, since this form was clearly dominant in working-class dialects of the southeast, including the capital Oslo.

After the 1938 reforms were implemented, certain people made the effort to count all the changes to the two standards, and the result was surprising to many: in a running text more alterations had been made to Nynorsk forms than to Bokmål. This was completely unacceptable to a number of Nynorsk supporters, since, they argued, Nynorsk was already both 'Norwegian' and, from its very beginning, was based on the popular dialects. Why then, they asked, had Nynorsk 'suffered' more changes than Bokmål, which was still marked by its Danish origins, and most of whose non-Danish features were based on upper-middle-class speech, not 'the people's language'?

One of the experts who had reviewed the Language Commission's recommendations before the reform was passed pointed to this frequency count and argued that this fact represented a serious problem for the entire set of reforms. Others did not agree and argued that Nynorsk supporters also had to make concessions in order for a pan-Norwegian standard to develop. Everyone accepted the idea that Nynorsk was based on popular dialects; however, many people pointed out that Aasen had drawn from the western dialects to a much greater degree than those in the southeast, and since the popular eastern dialects offered the most promising linguistic bridge between the two standards, Nynorsk, too, had to change dramatically (cf. Vaagland 1982). For Nynorsk this comprised merely a change in geographical focus – from west to east – while for Bokmål the changes were sociolinguistic in character, in principle shifting its base from upper-middle-class speech to popular eastern and working-class dialects.

The 1938 sociolinguistic experiment

The 1938 reforms represented a continuation of the 1917 reforms. Many of the optional elements introduced into Riksmål in 1917 were given a stronger position within the Bokmål standard, often as the sole acceptable forms, thereby relegating traditional, upper-middle-class speech forms to a secondary position, or even dropping them altogether. This reform package represented something new and revolutionary, an audacious sociolinguistic experiment: upper-middle-class speech was now defined as just one among many spoken varieties of Norwegian which the written Bokmål standard had to take into consideration. Upper-middle-class speech was no longer the normative base for written Bokmål; in fact, some upper-middle-class speech elements were for the first time labelled as non-standard, thus socially demoting the most prestigious spoken variety in the country.

Written Bokmål had thus been dragged across the salient sociolinguistic line between upper-middle-class speech and the popular rural and urban dialects. The language reform of 1938 was consistent with the ideology and sociolinguistic analysis of Halvdan Koht and the Labour Party, and with the declared aim of the majority in Parliament to pursue a pan-Norwegian compromise through continued language planning. It was perceived by the Riksmål supporters, and quite rightly so, as a working-class sociolinguistic revolution. From a socio-linguistic perspective, the 1938 reforms represent a unique language standardisation experiment.

Those with an upper-middle-class native dialect could no longer rely in all respects on their own spoken variety for writing correct standard Bokmål. The fact that the same applied to all other dialect speakers was an entirely different matter to them. Many upper-middle-class speakers, as well as people who were used to writing in the traditional Riksmål/Bokmål standard (of 1917), felt strongly that the entire 1938 reform package was an outrage against what they considered to be 'correct', 'nice' and 'proper' language. Defenders of this traditional standard decided to call the written standard they wanted to return to 'Riksmål', to distinguish it from the official 1938 Bokmål standard. The poet Arnulf Øverland (1889–1968) summed up their sentiments when he claimed that Bokmål after the 1938 reforms was 'not a language, but an insult' (Øverland 1948: 41, cf. also Øverland 1949).

The more traditional Nynorsk supporters were not pleased with the 1938 reforms either (Vaagland 1982). With Professor Gustav Indrebø (1889–1942) as their leader (cf. Venås 1984), supporters of conservative Nynorsk fought against what they considered to be the destruction of Nynorsk; they were especially furious about the first proposal from the commission in 1935 (published in January 1936). Their one achievement was that the final version of the 1938 reforms paid more attention to the Nynorsk standard's tradition than the commission had originally proposed. But there were also many Nynorsk advocates who defended the main idea behind the reforms, moving towards a pan-Norwegian standard. They were proven right in their conjecture that the reforms would work in favour of Nynorsk. Between 1938 and 1944, the percentage of schools choosing Nynorsk as their main standard increased from 22.0 per cent to 34.1 per cent (Torp and Vikør 1993: 209).

The fact that the use of Nynorsk expanded enormously after the 1938 reforms was not at all unexpected – this also happened after the reforms in 1907 and 1917 (Hovdan 1928). The part of the country where Nynorsk made the most gains in schools after 1938 was northern Norway. But, as we shall see, World War II had a huge impact on the very foundation of language debates and policy during the immediate post-war period.

Language in broadcasting

The question of language in the spoken media soon proved to be a problem, given the unique Norwegian language situation with no generally accepted spoken standard. No one in the 1930s argued that everyone should be free to speak their own local dialect when announcing programmes, presenting the news or giving the weather forecasts. During that period, the upper-middle-class spoken variety was viewed by its speakers, and probably by a majority of the population, as the obvious choice for the broadcast standard.

What really stirred up controversy in the 1930s concerning language use on the radio was the introduction of Nynorsk on the air. Hearing spoken Nynorsk was a totally new experience for most people. Many listeners claimed they could not understand it, and they wanted spoken Nynorsk to be banned from the radio (Dahl 1975: 297–308). This did not happen, of course, but a difficult question had to be solved by the broadcasters: how should spoken Nynorsk be pronounced on the air?

The solution was for presenters to utilise a close spelling pronunciation. A written Nynorsk text was therefore essential, and this further helped the view that a standardised version of spoken Nynorsk ought to follow the written standard as much as possible. While this may sound unproblematic, written Nynorsk (as well as written Bokmål) included so many optional and parallel forms that it was not such a clear-cut issue. Again, the solution was to opt for what were considered to be more or less mainstream Nynorsk forms that were not extreme in either a conservative sense ('Aasen-like') or a radical sense (closer to southeastern dialects or to Bokmål). This balance, however, was not always easy to achieve, and the issue continued to create public debate. For Bokmål, determining the radio standard was much easier: it had to be upper-middle-class speech, since that variety was more or less mirrored in mainstream written Riksmål/Bokmål at the time.

Parliament debated radio language use on several occasions during the 1930s, and their main conclusion was that the Norwegian Broadcasting Corporation's language policy should be to not offend or provoke the general public by being extreme in any sense. This principle may appear to be both reasonable and easy to put into practice, but there were a number of different avenues that could be followed to achieve it. One path was to direct presenters to use what could be considered a 'mainstream' pronunciation, as just mentioned. Alternatively, since upper-middle-class speech was looked upon by many listeners as being quite conservative and not at all in keeping with the goal of a pan-Norwegian standard, a Bokmål standard which was closer to Nynorsk would appear less 'extreme' than spoken Riksmål. There was obviously no clear solution to this problem.

Slowly, however, a practice based on a spelling pronunciation of both Nynorsk and Bokmål emerged as a practical way around the problem. This meant that after the 1938 reforms, Bokmål as used on the radio in news broadcasts, announcements and weather forecasts would no longer completely resemble upper-middle-class speech, since so many of its forms were now deemed to be non-standard. As one would expect, this was not acceptable to the Riksmål movement, which in the late 1940s and 1950s led a growing opposition movement against the way Bokmål was spoken on the radio.

The Nazi occupation of Norway and the Quisling Government's 1941 language reform

Norway was occupied by Nazi Germany between 1940 and 1945. During these five years, all previous civil disagreements between Norwegians were pushed aside in order to focus on mobilising resistance against the occupying forces. This affected the language struggle, too. The various language organisations gradually stopped functioning. However, at the beginning of the occupation a number of the leaders of *Riksmålsforbundet* disgraced themselves by appealing to the new authorities to abolish the 1938 language reforms (Tjelle 1994; Fløgstad 2004). This did not happen. Instead, the German-controlled Norwegian Government, headed by Vidkun Quisling (1887–1945), introduced its own language reforms in 1941. This had little influence on how people actually wrote during the war, even though the large-circulation nazified newspapers and dailies adopted the reforms. In the rhetoric of the Quisling Government, the main objective of the reform was to 'rectify' the written standards with regard to forms introduced as a result of the Labour Party's language programme.

The Nazi Government's language reform showed a clear conservative tendency in both standards. However, both during the war and after, this fact was overshadowed by the introduction in the Nazi reform of a few Nynorsk forms into Bokmål, especially the words *no* 'now' and *enno* 'still'. The compulsory use of the adverb *no* in Bokmål was described humorously in Oslo this way: '*Nå* skal *nu* hete *no!*' ('Now shall now be called now'), playing on the fact that *nå*, *nu* and *no* are three variants of the adverb 'now'. *Nå* was the most frequently used spoken form, particularly in the southeast, but at that time it lacked any solid tradition of use in either Bokmål or Nynorsk. *Nu* was the traditional Riksmål form inherited from written Danish, which also occurred in upper-middle-class speech (and in a few dialects). *No* was the traditional Nynorsk form, found in many local dialects.

Referring to the forms *no* and *enno*, the opponents of the 1938 reforms not infrequently claimed in the 1950s that the Nazis' language reforms represented another step in a pan-Norwegian direction. This was far from correct, and, in any case, the reform was largely sabotaged in the schools. The main result of the 1941 Nazi reform was an important side effect – for several years it prevented the 1938 reforms from being implemented. This happened because most Norwegians did not want to use word forms introduced by the Quisling Government, so they instead resorted to much older forms than those found in the 1938 standards. Only after the end of the war in 1945 could the 1938 standards really start being introduced properly.

Summary: the 'Oslo decision' of 1939

In the period between the two language reforms of 1917 and 1938, a pan-Norwegian standard was the politically desired result of language planning, and such a standard was perceived as representing a common linguistic system believed to unite all varieties of popular spoken Norwegian. To Halvdan Koht, this view represented a modification of Ivar Aasen's programme from the nineteenth century. Aasen had deliberately excluded the urban dialects, and to a large extent the rural southeastern dialects as well. But Aasen had carried out his main fieldwork in the 1840s, before the emergence of urban working-class dialects in the towns and cities.

The result of this process was that the Labour Party agreed with the language planning policy recommended by Koht: a pan-Norwegian standard achieved through opening up both written standards to the same popular forms and features from the dialects. The Labour Party adopted the slogan 'More room for the people's language' at their general convention in 1936 (Rykkja 1978: 176).

For the period 1915–40, we need to distinguish between two groups in Parliament who supported a pan-Norwegian solution. The first faction saw a pan-Norwegian standard as a reasonable solution to the problem caused by the rise of and competition between the two national written standards – the outcome of the language reforms in 1917 and of the entire first period of language planning after 1814. They were probably in a large majority within the pan-Norwegian block in Parliament. The second, smaller, group saw the pan-Norwegian policy as a means to politically unite and socially elevate the working and peasant classes. Their view thus had an obvious sociopolitical and ideological foundation, supporting Halvdan Koht's analysis and policy. The pan-Norwegian policy to them was far more than a mere solution to a language problem – it was a vehicle with which to further a desired political development through language planning.

The 1938 reform was consistent with the language planning policy now endorsed by the Labour Party. Its main objective was the politically motivated demotion of upper-middle-class speech from serving as the only basis for the development and standardisation of the Bokmål standard. The 1907 and 1917 reforms of Riksmål (later Bokmål) followed the direction outlined by Knudsen in the nineteenth century of Norwegianising written Danish by using upper-middle-class speech as the basis for the development. But with the parallel creation and subsequent development of a competing standard, Landsmål (later Nynorsk), the pressing problem was to ensure that a single standard emerged in the future. The pan-Norwegian solution seemed to be a reasonable compromise to many politicians. However, what was not understood by everybody was that in order to reach such a compromise, a sociolinguistic revolution was necessary. Bokmål had to be forced across the most important sociolinguistic line in Norwegian society, that between upper-middle-class speech and the popular dialects. In the first half of the 1930s, the Labour Party embraced Koht's analysis and language planning policy of working towards a pan-Norwegian solution using 'the people's language' as the normative base. Their 1938 reforms followed up and effectively executed this policy.

In 1939, at the Labour Party's initiative, the Oslo School Board adopted a resolution to the effect that word forms which were common to both Bokmål and Nynorsk in the 1938 standards were to be included in the textbooks used in Oslo schools. Several school boards in other areas followed Oslo's example (Hoel 2011: 435). The consequence of the 'Oslo resolution' was that Bokmål textbooks after the war used more sociolinguistically radical forms than necessary. The language used in these school books thus deviated considerably from the spoken upper-middle-class variety, leaning in the direction of a pan-Norwegian merger of Bokmål and Nynorsk. The Oslo market was important for the publishing houses. Therefore, school books in general – not only for Oslo but for the whole country – followed the practice in Oslo, and after this decision were often written in a standard Bokmål variety which was soon branded 'pan-Norwegian' (*samnorsk*) by the many people who were utterly dismayed at the language found in the textbooks. After the war, the very concept of 'pan-Norwegian' acquired a different meaning. This was due to massive agitation by Riksmål supporters, who consistently used 'Samnorsk' as a derogatory term for the Bokmål variety with the least number of word forms taken from upper-middle-class speech, as found in school textbooks as a consequence of the 'Oslo resolution'.

Thus, the scene was set for a fierce language struggle in the late 1940s and throughout the 1950s into the 1960s. Riksmål supporters wanted to reverse the sociolinguistic experiment, or revolution, of 1938 and put an end to the language planning policy in which 'the people's language' was defined as the norm. The objective of Riksmål activists was to return to a stage in language planning where written Bokmål would again mirror upper-middle-class speech. The 'obligatory Riksmål' standard of 1917 represented such a stage.

CHAPTER 7

The post-war language struggle (1945–66) to counter the sociolinguistic experiment of 1938

Political developments from 1945 to 1965

Following Norway's liberation from German occupation in May 1945, national elections were held in the autumn in which the Labour Party won a solid majority of seats in Parliament and subsequently formed a government. It kept this majority throughout the 1940s and 1950s, until 1961. This period was dominated domestically by a policy of rebuilding the country after the war. Norway's foreign policy was heavily influenced by the Cold War, and it joined the NATO alliance in 1949. In the 1961 election, the Labour Party lost its absolute majority in Parliament, but, together with a smaller party to the political left, it held a tiny majority of seats. However, in 1965 the Labour Government resigned after losing to a coalition of more non-socialist parties that were able to form a new majority government.

The post-war language political situation

During the five war years, 1940–5, the language conflict was pushed into the background and was dwarfed by the struggle against the German occupation forces. After liberation, pre-war political conflicts resurfaced. However, it soon became apparent that the war had caused a profound change in the underlying premises of the language struggle.

In a Gallup poll carried out in 1946, four out of five Norwegians

Figure 7.1   Arnulf Øverland (1889–1968), photo. (Source: unknown/National Library of Norway.)

surveyed said that they supported the rapid development of a pan-Norwegian standard (*Aftenposten* 3 May 1946); however, the way this was to be achieved was not mentioned in the question. It is reasonable to credit this result as stemming from the general post-war feeling that it was necessary to work together to rebuild all aspects of Norwegian life and to seek compromise and cooperation between former political adversaries. This also applied to the language situation, where a single pan-Norwegian standard seemed to be a way out of the lengthy language struggle which had begun in the middle of the previous century.

During the war, Arnulf Øverland wrote many influential poems which encapsulated the population's sentiments at the time. After the war, Øverland managed to reorganise and revive the Riksmål movement. In order to achieve this, it proved important that he was acknowledged in society at large as an ideological hero of the national resistance movement. He led the Riksmål movement into a struggle not against Nynorsk, which – and this was new – Øverland accepted as a fully developed cultural standard, but rather against the idea of a pan-Norwegian standard (*samnorsk*) (Taule 1973). The very term 'Samnorsk' soon came to signify the 1938 variety of Bokmål which incorporated many of the popular low-status and working-class dialect forms introduced into Bokmål in the reforms of 1917 and 1938. The more official term for this written variety was 'Radical Bokmål' (*radikalt bokmål*). The term 'Samnorsk' therefore came to signify an already existing official variety of Bokmål – and not a future pan-Norwegian solution, which had been the pre-war meaning of the term. It was against the use of Radical Bokmål in school textbooks that the Riksmål movement, under Øverland's leadership, directed its attacks from the late 1940s onwards.

The fight to restore the lost normative role of upper-middle-class speech – a sociolinguistic counter-revolution – had begun.

The counting reform (1951)

As has been demonstrated, the final word about Norwegian language planning and language standardisation lies with Parliament. This principle was established in 1919 with reference to the 1917 reforms. Since then, it has been taken more or less for granted that every language planning reform had to be decided upon by Parliament.

Although Parliament had dealt a number of times with oral language in the schools, almost every discussion and decision about specific language developments was focused on the written standards. The only time that Parliament made a decision about spoken forms happened in 1950. This reform, implemented in 1951, profoundly changed the deeply-rooted counting system for numbers over twenty.

The matter itself had nothing to do with the language struggle as such, since it had no bearing on the issue of Bokmål versus Nynorsk or on a pan-Norwegian standard. However, to the many people opposed to the official state policy of working towards a pan-Norwegian solution, this case only added to the frustration over what they considered to be the state's interference in an area with which it should not be involved in the first place, namely language planning and standardisation.

In 1950, the telephone company in Oslo needed to replace five-digit phone numbers with six-digit numbers. In Norwegian, as in German and Danish, compound numbers above twenty were read aloud with the units given before the tens: for example, 26 was six-and-twenty. Norwegians recite telephone numbers as pairs of digits, so a six-digit number such as 21–54–93 would be read as one-and-twenty, four-and-fifty, three-and-ninety. It was pointed out that many people were phoning wrong numbers because the operators read out the pairs of number in the reverse order to how they should be dialled. The reform was to read the numbers out as pairs in the actual order of the digits: for example, twenty-one, fifty-four, ninety-three.

Having begun as a recommendation by the telephone company, this counting reform was passed by the government in March 1950 and eventually ended up as a matter for Parliament, which approved the change by a large majority. The Ministry of Church and Education then decreed that 'the new method of counting' was to be taught in schools from the autumn of 1951 and used by the government administration and the Norwegian Broadcasting Corporation from the summer of 1951 onwards.

It is interesting to note that one of the arguments put forward in favour of the reform was that the new counting system was more 'international' than the old one. This shows how fundamentally reoriented Norway had become after World War II. Previously, Denmark and Germany – and thus Danish and German – had been the closest and most obvious reference points for Norway and Norwegian, but now Swedish and English had overtaken them. Danish and German mirrored the 'old' Norwegian counting system, while Swedish and English mirrored the 'new' system.

The Norwegian-American linguist Einar Haugen (1906–94) was in Norway when the reform was adopted, and reported later that he:

> noted that at first a number of adults made a deliberate effort to use the new system. But ten years later, when again visiting Norway, he [Einar Haugen] found that after energetic teaching in the public schools the new usage was still confined almost entirely to those who were officially obliged to use it: state broadcasters and school children. Practically no adults were using it, including the girls in the telephone exchange, and school children appeared to drop it when they became adults. Nevertheless, it will undoubtedly become rooted in Norwegian speech some day, but no one can say how long it will take. It is an interesting illustration of the resistance which language makes to even the most obviously logical changes. Perhaps the general atmosphere of language reform in Norway had induced an over-optimistic attitude with respect to the possibility of inculcating new linguistic habits. (Haugen 1966a: 188f.)

Developments from 1951 onwards are indeed interesting from a sociolinguistic perspective. Haugen's prediction that 'some day' the 'new way of counting' will be rooted in Norwegian speech has proved to be right, but perhaps not in the exact way Haugen thought it would. Today, it seems that Norwegians use both counting systems. However, usage varies according to well-known sociolinguistic features: age, social class, education, level of formality, and so on. Various studies have shown a general tendency that the more education individuals have, the higher their social class, and the more formal the situation, the more frequently they use the new system. It is worth noting that the current (2013) Norwegian Prime Minister, Jens Stoltenberg (born in 1959), is rather consistent in using the old system, while many of his ministers are equally consistent in using the new system.

In 1951, many of those in favour of the new counting system thought that the older one would vanish completely. This optimism about imposing changes on the spoken language shows a lack of understanding about how successful language planning can be. Given the government's success up to that point in directing and changing the written standards, it is perhaps not difficult to see how they could misjudge the possibility of altering the spoken language. But there are only a few documented cases worldwide of successful language planning for oral varieties; the abolition of the Icelandic *flámæli* pronunciation is perhaps the best known (Jahr 1989a).

A permanent Language Committee (1952)

Much of the conflict in the 1950s was centred around the Norwegian Language Committee (*Norsk språknemnd*), which was established in 1952 following a parliamentary resolution the year before, and was tasked with developing a pan-Norwegian standard 'on the basis of the people's language'. The Riksmål movement was completely opposed to the Committee's mandate, claiming that it was 'restricted'. The Language Committee consisted of thirty members, fifteen representing each main standard. The members were appointed by the government and were experts in Norwegian, native-language teaching, fiction writing and the media. The main political rationale behind the Language Committee was clearly to try and wrest the problematic language issue away from politicians and delegate it to a board of experts. (Christensen 2009: 36. On the establishment of the Language Committee, see Hellevik 1964.)

However, this attempt failed. Indeed, because of its mandate, the establishment of, and subsequent work by, the Language Committee generated even more controversy and turmoil, and politicians had to deal with the language question for another half-century.

The post-war 'Riksmål' norm of 1952

As a consequence, an unofficial variety of Bokmål came into use, one that reflected upper-middle-class speech exactly and was in principle identical with the traditional Riksmål standard after the 1917 reforms (that is, Riksmål with 'obligatory' forms). It was even called 'Riksmål' by its supporters. This private variety avoided the feminine gender and included older forms such as *frem, nu, sprog, syd, efter, sne, farve*. However, it did accept several of the purely orthographic changes introduced into Bokmål in 1938: for example, *-øi- > -øy-, mig > meg* 'me', *dig > deg* 'you', *blandt > blant* 'among', *op > opp* 'up', *gjennem > gjennom* 'through', *mellem > mellom* 'between'; all of the accepted forms were the same as the Nynorsk spellings. This unofficial Riksmål standard competed successfully with official Standard Bokmål from the early 1950s onwards, especially in the media and private enterprise. Several of the most prominent contemporary authors and poets actively used and supported this unofficial standard.

And the picture is even more complicated than that, since official Standard Bokmål was itself divided into two competing varieties, as we saw earlier. Bokmål therefore now came in three varieties, each reflecting a different degree of incorporation of southeastern and working-class dialect forms and thus different sociolinguistic bases:

- *Conservative Bokmål*: with no working-class forms, reflecting upper-middle-class speech, but unofficial since important features lay outside the Standard Bokmål of 1938; this variety was referred to as 'Riksmål'.
- *Moderate Bokmål*: with as few working-class forms as possible, but still falling within the official standard of 1938.
- *Radical Bokmål*: with as many working-class (or pan-Norwegian) forms as possible within the official Bokmål standard, approaching Standard Nynorsk.

The Riksmål movement's resistance through the 1950s

Throughout the entire post-war period up to the end of the 1960s, the Riksmål movement was to a large extent allowed to dominate in the media and the public sphere generally. The 1950s was a time when political and social considerations – which in the pre-war period had been basic in the language question – were not so much at the forefront of the debate. Halvdan Koht's pre-war class-based motivation for pursuing a pan-Norwegian standard had more or less vanished. The political right and private enterprise supported the Riksmål movement, private enterprise contributed to it financially, among other ways by advertising in every issue of the Riksmål movement's publications *Frisprog* (*Free Language*) and *Ordet* (*The Word*).

The Riksmål movement's success in redefining the term 'Samnorsk' as equivalent to Radical Bokmål, rather than being a pan-Norwegian target for language planning, showed quite convincingly that the political motivation behind developing a pan-Norwegian standard was no longer being defended effectively by the Labour Party or the government. Arguments in support of a pan-Norwegian strategy became non-political in nature and were restricted to merely practical and financial concerns: that is, that it was too costly and problematic to sustain two national standards of Norwegian.

This line of argument was far from sufficient to withstand the variety of opposing arguments offered by the Riksmål movement. They were defending the written tradition dating back to the great poets and authors of the nineteenth century: Henrik Wergeland, Henrik Ibsen, Bjørnstjerne Bjørnson. They launched hard-hitting attacks on southeastern and working-class features found in Radical Bokmål as being 'vulgar', making a point that these forms often stood out stylistically as alien elements in written texts. Moreover, they emerged as defenders of the individual's right to choose his or her language variety, a right they argued they were being deprived of by the state.

Riksmål supporters could neither understand nor accept the fact that the written standard they considered to be their language no longer allowed some of the word forms that they had been taught were 'correct', 'educated' and 'proper'. They saw it as totally unacceptable that the current official written Bokmål standard required their children to use forms which they had always considered 'sloppy', 'ugly' or even 'vulgar'. Riksmål supporters could not or would not recognise that this viewpoint implied the social denigration of speakers who used these so-called 'vulgar' forms in their everyday speech. The Riksmål movement organised extensive resistance to the authorities' attempts to further the development of a pan-Norwegian standard. Although this opposition originated in the western upper-class districts of Oslo, it rapidly spread far outside the capital, and soon followers were recruited from more or less the entire country.

The Riksmål movement resented the political and sociolinguistic aims of Koht and the Labour Party to promote the use in writing of forms found in the everyday speech of a vast majority of the Norwegian people. Riksmål supporters saw their struggle as primarily a fight against the state dictating how they should write their own language, and they argued vehemently for what they termed a 'free development of language' (*fri sprogutvikling*), meaning no involvement at all by the state or political authorities in language planning. That such a situation would exclusively promote their high-status upper-middle-class spoken variety was something they were not willing to admit. The sociolinguistic aspect of the conflict was obvious, but mostly denied by the Riksmål supporters.

The Riksmål movement's opposition to low-status ('radical') forms in textbooks was formidable and appeared in many guises. 'The parents' campaign against pan-Norwegian' (begun in 1951) originated on the west side of Oslo but received support from large areas of the country (Guttu 2007). Their actions took on many forms: letters to editors, posters or newspaper advertisements, petitions and demonstrations. In 1953, parents of pupils in the western districts of Oslo initiated a campaign of 'correcting' school textbooks. In some classes, nearly all the pupils' books had, for example, the feminine gender definite singular ending -a corrected in pen to common gender -en: for example musa ('the mouse') was changed to musen; dokka ('the doll') to dukken; ei ('a', fem. sg. indef. art.) to en; and so on (cf. Fig. 7.2, p. 137).

In 1954, the Oslo School Board yielded to pressure from the Parents' Campaign, and altered its 1939 'Oslo resolution'. Moderate Bokmål forms were introduced into Oslo schools, and this gradually influenced textbooks all over the country.

The language conflict intensified throughout the 1950s and into the 1960s, affecting all domains in which the language question surfaced, not just schools. The opposition argued effectively that the authorities were actually destroying the main variety of Norwegian, which the Riksmål supporters used to consider 'their' language. Local referenda were still important in determining which standard was used in schools, and in certain areas Riksmål supporters mobilised to vote Nynorsk out of the school districts. This occurred despite Øverland's statement that the Riksmål movement would make peace with Nynorsk in their struggle against what they now considered their main enemy: pan-Norwegian.

The language used by the Norwegian Broadcasting Corporation (NRK) was certainly part of this conflict in the 1950s. The Norwegian Authors' Association was split on the question of whether it should be represented on the Language Committee. A minority of its members – many of whom were well-known authors who did not want their association to have anything to do with the Committee – left and formed their own Riksmål association of authors. This operated until 1966, when it rejoined the Norwegian Authors' Association.

Some of the means employed by the Riksmål supporters in their struggle were very insensitive. For instance, only a decade or two after Nazi atrocities had taken place in the country, young high-school Riksmål supporters threw school textbooks onto bonfires because they were written in Radical Bokmål, which was branded as 'pan-Norwegian' by Riksmål advocates. The first of these book burnings occurred in 1956, the final in 1963 (Vinje 1978: 380). Many Riksmål supporters were not able to see that this was a totally unacceptable form of action, with unpleasant recent associations. The poet André Bjerke (1918–85), one of their ideological leaders and the founder and editor of their magazine *Ordet*, actually wrote enthusiastically about this deed – one of his articles carried the title 'Books as fuel for the bonfire!' (Bjerke [1963] 1968).

Even though Riksmål advocates at the time did not always recognise that their cause was steadily gaining ground, the high level of activity and vast resources marshalled in its support by businesses and private individuals paid off politically in the long run. The repeated and lasting attacks on the authorities regarding the language question caused the ruling Labour Party to gradually view its identification with the pan-Norwegian policy as a negative factor which might eventually bring down the government.

Pan-Norwegian supporters organise too late

Only when the battle over the pan-Norwegian strategy had in reality been lost was the first pan-Norwegian organisation since *Østlandsk reisning* founded – The National League for Language Unification (*Landslaget for språklig samling*), in 1959. This group gained quite a substantial following in its first years, but then rapidly faded away. The League was not sufficiently influential to counter the dismantling of the pan-Norwegian policy which started in the early 1960s. Moreover, the organisation was perceived as arguing for a more technical or 'non-political' solution to the two-standard situation, namely that a pan-Norwegian standard should be constructed as a linguistic compromise between the already existing Nynorsk and Bokmål standards. It was not until the mid-1970s, when it no longer held any influence except for two seats on the Language Council (cf. below), that this organisation began to argue along the ideological lines of the 1920s and 1930s – that is, it adopted the ideas associated with *Østlandsk reisning* and Halvdan Koht (Strand 1979; Vannebo 1979; Vikør and Wiggen 1979).

MURR SATT PÅ LUR.

SÅ KOM EN MUS

UT AV ET H̶Ö̶L̶ ᴴᵁᴸᴸ

I EN MUR.

MURR SLO

MED S̶t̶ ˢⁱⁿ KLO.

OG SNIPP, SNAPP, SNUTE,

SÅ VAR MUS̶A̶ ᵉⁿ UTE.

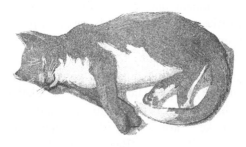

Figure 7.2   Copy of a page from an ABC book from an Oslo school 1953/1954.
(Note: the text is corrected in pen by a parent from official Bokmål (called 'pan-
Norwegian' by the Riksmål movement and supporters) to the private Riksmål
standard with upper-middle-class speech forms. The three-gender system of
standard Bokmål is replaced by a two-gender system (*ei* > *en* 'a', *si* > *sin* 'its',
musa > *musen* 'the mouse'), and the word form *hol* 'hole' (similar to the Nynorsk
form and also related to the southeastern and working-class dialect form *høl*) is
changed to the upper-middle-class form *hull*.)

Different ideologies within the language political camps

The post-war Nynorsk movement was divided into two main ideological camps. The side which clearly represented the majority of
Nynorsk supporters at the time accepted that Bokmål was now a
national standard. Many of them supported the pan-Norwegian

policy, arguing that it was necessary to secure as much of written Nynorsk as possible in the future pan-Norwegian standard (Skard 1963). The other camp continued to use the dominant arguments of the nationalist period and would not accept that Bokmål represented a genuinely national standard. It considered the traditional written Landsmål standard of 1917 to be the ultimate standard to defend, and they did not want to have anything to do with the changes made in 1938 (Kvamen 1958).

The Riksmål weekly newspaper, *Frisprog*, reported enthusiastically whenever Nynorsk was voted out as the main standard in a school district and replaced with Bokmål. Such events were invariably viewed as telling victories for the Riksmål cause, regardless of how displeased most of the Riksmål supporters usually were with the official Bokmål standard. However, the Riksmål movement was also divided, with two sides taking a different main focus in their opposition to the official pan-Norwegian policy. One faction, clearly the biggest and the politically dominant one, argued that it was undemocratic of the state authorities to pursue a pan-Norwegian policy against such strong opposition. They demanded a general referendum to settle the language question once and for all, claiming that the majority should rule in questions concerning linguistic issues. They also claimed, surprisingly enough, that a majority of the population actually had to memorise which nouns belonged to the feminine gender. Their knowlegde of spoken varieties outside of upper-middle-class Oslo speech was clearly quite limited (Bjerke 1960; Hjort 1963).

The other side of the Riksmål movement was dominated by people with more linguistic knowledge and understanding who knew very well that the feminine gender occurred in all Norwegian dialects except in Bergen and in upper-middle-class speech. They accepted Nynorsk as a literatary and cultural standard. Their views were founded on the fact that all the various spoken varieties, as well as traditional written Nynorsk and Riksmål, represented unique structural systems. Thus, they considered it wrong, and even impossible, to interfere with the traditional written Riksmål standard as it was based on the linguistic system of spoken Riksmål. Their arguments in favour of the Riksmål standard were clearly more linguistically sophisticated and had their scholarly basis in the structuralist framework of de Saussure and the Prague School. In *Frisprog*, their viewpoints were most often expressed in longer and more argumentative articles and pieces (Riksmålsvernet 1958, cf. especially comments by Carl Hjalmar Borgstrøm and Ingerid Dal; Dal 1963a, 1963b.)

The supporters of pan-Norwegian could also be said to have consisted of two groups with a slightly different focus on how to reach the goal of a pan-Norwegian written standard, although this difference of opinion was less openly expressed in the public debate. One group wanted to achieve this goal rapidly and argued that it was possible to construct a common standard based entirely on the contemporary Bokmål and Nynorsk standards. What was needed, in their view, was just a technical adjustment process, and a decision about which forms should be selected as the pan-Norwegian forms (*Framlegg* 1966). The other pan-Norwegian group argued more in line with the pre-war perspective of Halvdan Koht and the Labour Party of the 1930s that a pan-Norwegian policy and subsequent standard had to be developed gradually through the necessary influx into the Bokmål standard of previously low-status spoken dialect forms (southeastern and working-class), as well as forms which coincided with those of Nynorsk. Importing such forms into the written Bokmål standard in order to increase their overall social status was seen as more important than reaching a rapid pan-Norwegian solution. Over the course of the late 1940s and 1950s, the Labour Party clearly shifted from the latter, more ideological position to the former, more technical position (Skirbekk 1967; Jahr 1992).

The Smebye case: no standardisation in the spoken media

The new method of counting in the spoken language was a specific, one-off decision. Another unique case illustrates the fundamental, predominant 'hands-off' attitude in Norway to spoken as opposed to written language. The authorities' view was that for certain radio programmes such as the news and weather, only official Bokmål forms from the 1938 standard, or Nynorsk, were to be used. However, a well-known weatherman, Sigurd Jahr Smebye (1922–85), referred to as the 'abominable snowman', insisted on using his own upper-middle-class variety ('spoken Riksmål') when reporting on the weather. This involved only a few problematic forms, for example *sne* instead of Standard Bokmål *snø* ('snow', this gave rise to his special nickname), *syd* for *sør* ('south'), *frem* for *fram* ('forward'), *nu* rather than *nå* ('now'), *efter* instead of *etter* ('after'). All the standard forms were branded by the Riksmål movement as typical pan-Norwegian features, and so Smebye refused to use them during his radio broadcasts.

The Smebye case generated a great deal of discussion in 1955 and 1956 and turned into a heated debate. However, it was not until February 1962 that Smebye received a letter from the ministry responsible for the broadcast media informing him that he was relieved of his duty of reading the weather forecasts, since he refused to follow the official Bokmål standard and insisted on using disallowed upper-middle-class speech forms.

Smebye took the case to court, supported by the now very powerful Riksmål movement, which considered him a champion of their cause. Smebye argued that even though he had not suffered any decrease in salary nor lost his job, he nevertheless felt discriminated against for using his own natural spoken language when reading the weather forecasts. In October 1963, the Oslo District Court ruled that there was no legal basis for the ministry's action, since language planning and the standardisation of Bokmål and Nynorsk applied only to the written and not the spoken language. The court stated that the ministry was wrong to make reference to the official Bokmål standard as the basis for its decision.

The Riksmål movement celebrated this outcome as a great victory over the government and its language policy. The authorities also regarded it in the same way, and only a few months later the government set up the Language Peace Committee (cf. below).

In reality, however, there was no real reason for Riksmål supporters to celebrate in this particular case. The court's ruling was in keeping with a principle that the Riksmål movement had always resented: the 1878 resolution about free use of dialect in schools, which, as we have seen, was incorporated into the School Act in 1915 and 1917. This meant that there would not be any spoken standard taught in schools, and consequently no spoken standard could be established and accepted by society at large as 'standard spoken Norwegian'. The Riksmål movement always considered their spoken variety of Norwegian to be the standard; therefore, in reality, they misinterpreted the ruling of the court as a victory for their cause. Instead, it was more of a victory for the view that in Norway there is no spoken standard, only written standards, and therefore the authorities have no legal basis for demanding the use of specific pronunciations or spoken word forms that are unnatural to a language user. In principle, this ruling was valid for any dialect speaker as well as for users of the upper-middle-class spoken variety.

However, even given the court's ruling about the Smebye case in 1963, radio and television presenters of news broadcasts have mostly adhered to using written Bokmål or Nynorsk standard forms. It was not until 2010 that a dialect-speaking news anchor, Ingerid Stenvold (b. 1977, from northern Norway), presented the news on national television. This reflected both the 1878 principle (free use of dialect in schools) and also the Smebye ruling (free use of an individual's spoken variety on radio and TV). When the director of the Norwegian Broadcasting Corporation rejected protests about Stenvold's use of her local dialect while presenting the news on television, he was in perfect compliance with history, as well as with Norwegian language planning policy dating back more than a century.

The New Textbook Standard (1959)

The most important task of the Language Committee was to prepare a new textbook standard. The Committee's task was to suggest which of the many parallel forms introduced into Standard Bokmål and Standard Nynorsk in the 1938 reforms should be used in textbooks. The intention was that a narrower standard would provide school books with a linguistic norm that was 'in the middle', that is neither very conservative nor very radical, and therefore would render parallel editions of school books with 'moderate' and 'radical' forms superfluous. The New Textbook Standard (*Ny læreboknormal*) was proposed by the Language Committee in 1957. Against vigorous protests from both conservative Riksmål supporters and conservative Nynorsk supporters, Parliament accepted the Committee's revised proposal in 1959.

The Language Peace Commission (1964–6)

The 1959 textbook standard appeared to signal that the pan-Norwegian strategy would continue. But in reality the language planning policy aimed at a pan-Norwegian solution had already been abandoned. The Labour Party leaders now wanted to be free from a binding commitment to a pan-Norwegian standard. The party preferred to transfer the language issue from the political scene to a body of experts. But there had been too much unrest associated with the Language Committee's recommendations for it to be transformed into such a body. The Labour Party leaders no longer wanted the burden of heading the efforts towards reconciling the two standards, and without active support from the Labour Party, the pan-Norwegian policy was doomed.

Several secret meetings were held in the early 1960s between leaders of the Riksmål movement and the Labour Party, as well as with central figures from other political parties (Bull 1980: 250). This led – in January 1964 – to the government appointing an *ad hoc* political commission that was to survey and discuss all problems concerning the language conflict. This commission was referred to as the 'Vogt Commission', after its chairman, the linguist and President of the University of Oslo, Hans Vogt (1903–86). It was also known as 'The Language Peace Commission', since it was given a mandate to propose mechanisms that were to serve as the basis for reconciliation between the various parties of the language struggle. The commission was asked 'to evaluate the entire language situation and recommend measures which may serve to protect and develop our Norwegian linguistic heritage'. Two of the nine commission members represented the Riksmål movement, a fact which clearly indicated that the government's objective now was to find a way out of the language planning policy which had been pursued since about 1915, that is a pan-Norwegian solution.

The commission delivered its report in April 1966, after the Labour Government had resigned and been replaced by a coalition administration consisting of non-socialist parties. The report was immediately sent out to numerous institutions and associations which were asked to give their opinion on the recommendations.

The most substantial and, later, controversial point in the commission's report was a statement (on p. 31) concerning forms from upper-middle-class speech that had been defined as non-standard in the 1938 reform: 'In principal, it is unfortunate that forms which have traditionally been used in the written language, and which are still in common use in literature and speech, are excluded from the official written [Bokmål] standard' (*Innstilling* 1966: 53). This statement clearly signalled the Riksmål movement's victory in the post-war period.

In addition, the commission recommended that the permanent

thirty-member Language Committee be disbanded and replaced by an even larger Language Council with a mandate which comprised the Riksmål movement's principle view: it should have no ambition to initiate language changes through language planning, but instead follow and record how actual language use developed, and base its language standardisation proposals on this factor alone.

This report by the 'Language Peace Commission', which was very much in favour of the Riksmål agenda, marks the end of the language struggle's post-war period. The main objective of the Riksmål movement had been to counter the sociolinguistic experiment introduced through the 1938 reforms. The groundwork was now prepared for a rapid reinstatement of the upper-middle-class speech forms which had been dropped from the Bokmål standard in 1938. However, before this could happen, the entire political situation and priorities changed, and new political ideas emerged from the events of 1968 in Paris, the USA and Prague. The early 1970s witnessed a profound change in perspective among many young people in Norway. This meant that the language struggle changed course once more, leading to a different type of Norwegian language planning policy.

The post-war Nynorsk situation

During the war years (1940–5), there had been little opportunity for the use of Nynorsk in wider society. The Nynorsk movement suffered a serious setback from this, as well as from the fact that the entire archive of *Noregs Mållag* was destroyed in a fire in 1944. When peace arrived in 1945, the Nynorsk movement had to start almost from scratch, despite its continued gains in schools since the 1938 reforms.

The nationalist argument that Nynorsk was more 'Norwegian' than Bokmål, and that those people who used and supported Nynorsk were more patriotic than those who did not, was also no longer viable. Having a 'national' attitude during the war meant not siding with Nazi Germany or the Norwegian Nazi Party; it did not involve the question of whether a person was in favour of either Nynorsk or Bokmål. The basis for the old nationalist criticism of 'the two cultures' gradually disappeared over the course of the war.

Supporters of the Nynorsk movement therefore had to marshal quite different arguments than before in favour of their standard. But

several decades passed before the Nynorsk movement as a whole recognised this, and, in the meantime, the Nynorsk standard lost ground
constantly, especially as the main standard in elementary schools. The
percentage of schoolchildren who had Nynorsk as their first language
dropped on average by half a point every year following 1944, when
it was about one-third of the total number of schoolchildren in the
country, until the mid-1970s, by which time it had decreased to
around 16.5 per cent (Torp and Vikør 1993: 209).

As a result of this decline, in which a program of school centralisa-
tion in the 1950s also played a major part, and an inability among
the Nynorsk supporters to find new convincing arguments to use in
the language debate, an internal and long-lasting disagreement arose
within the Nynorsk movement. This was hardly surprising, as a lack
of external success often leads to attempts to find internal causes.

For many years the Nynorsk movement had been divided into conflicting ideological branches, as we have already seen. The clash was
the strongest between those individuals who supported traditional
Nynorsk (the pre-1938 variety) and those who welcomed the 1938
reforms and wanted to continue working towards a pan-Norwegian
solution. The traditionalists argued that the other group represented
a defeatist line with respect to Bokmål. The pan-Norwegian supporters claimed that their view was the only realistic one for the situation
as it was developing. They asserted that with the rapid decline of
Nynorsk as the main standard in schools, and with the difficulty they
were having in arguing effectively in favour of Nynorsk, it had become
important to work to secure as much of the Nynorsk standard as
possible into the future pan-Norwegian standard.

However, traditionalists continued to maintain their view that the
Nynorsk standard should be promoted as before. They interpreted
the reduced support for Nynorsk after the war as a direct result of
the linguistic changes introduced into Nynorsk in 1938, and wanted
to reverse these. However, yet another group of Nynorsk supporters
disagreed with both of these viewpoints and took a third position:
that as a result of the 1938 reforms, Nynorsk was now better suited
as a written medium for all local dialects, including the southeastern
dialects. They did not want to return to a more traditional Nynorsk
standard, and they did not see themselves as supporters of pan-
Norwegian; rather, they felt the Nynorsk standard had now found its
final suitable form in the 1938 reforms.

Summary: the post-war period

The language struggle from 1945 to 1966 stands out as a period in which the language question was discussed and dealt with as a separate issue from the general political and social questions of the time. During the previous and, as we will see, following periods, the language issue was integrated into the general political ideologies of the time, but this was much less so in the immediate post-war era. This made it surprisingly easy for the Riksmål movement to dominate the public scene completely. The Nynorsk movement found it very difficult to counteract this new situation effectively. The result was internal disagreement and conflict within the Nynorsk movement, and a steady decline throughout the whole period in the use of Nynorsk in primary-school districts.

Riksmål advocates, starting at the end of the 1940s, were very successful in their counter-attacks on the sociolinguistic experiment inherent in the official language planning policy, even though most of them did not seem to be aware of the fact that the authorities were giving in to their demands. The establishment of a non-official Riksmål standard in 1952 was very important as it gave the Riksmål movement something to argue and work *for*, not only something to argue against. But with the exception of the decision in 1954 by the Oslo School Board to abandon Radical Bokmål in school textbooks, Riksmål supporters did not have many concrete victories to celebrate. However, their well-supported and generously funded repeated attacks on the authorities over the language question finally paid off when the Labour Party in essence abandoned their pan-Norwegian policy.

The arguments presented in the post-war period by the Riksmål supporters were not challenged effectively. The Nynorsk movement was busily occupied with its own internal affairs during these years, and the supporters of a pan-Norwegian standard did not organise their forces well. This was probably because they trusted that the programme of developing a pan-Norwegian solution could not be stopped, as they felt it was the only reasonable solution to the problem of two competing written standards. They also believed that the government and Parliament were firmly determined to follow this policy to its conclusion.

To many people, the New Textbook Standard of 1959 signalled

that the pan-Norwegian policy would continue. This, however, was a false impression. The leaders of the Labour Party were afraid that opponents of the pan-Norwegian policy could bring the government down. The Labour Party leaders therefore wanted to disconnect the language question from the political scene, which they accomplished by establishing the 'Language Peace Commission' which functioned between 1964 and 1966.

Without active support from the Labour Party, the pan-Norwegian policy, as it had been envisioned by Halvdan Koht and the Labour Party in the 1930s, could not succeed. And in any case, in 1966 Labour was no longer the party of government. A new administration had taken over, the Vietnam War was starting to make its influence felt on young people's political ideologies, and new ideas would soon emerge to change the entire post-war framework within which the language struggle had been fought.

FROM A SINGLE-STANDARD TO A TWO-STANDARD STRATEGY

The end of the single-standard policy (1966–2002): reforms in 1981 and 2005 (for Bokmål) and 2012 (for Nynorsk)

Political developments from 1965 to 2013

The non-socialist government which took charge in 1965 was replaced by a Labour government in 1971 as a result of inner tensions among the coalition parties over the question of Norway seeking membership of the European Community (EC). Throughout the period 1971 to 2005, Labour and non-socialist governments came and went. All together there were fifteen changes of government – most of them minority administrations or involving coalitions of many different parties – five of these lasted only one year before falling. From 2005 up to today (2013), a coalition between Labour and two smaller parties has been in power.

Norwegian society changed dramatically during the 1970s and 1980s. The post-war period was definitively over. When the post-war baby-boom generation came of age an increasing number of young people sought higher education. This led to the establishment of new universities and university colleges. The number of students attending these higher education institutions was approximately 10,000 in 1960, had trebled to 30,000 in 1970, and by 1980 had reached 74,000. In 1986, university student enrolment stood at 103,000, and, for the first time, female students were in the majority (Nielsen 2011: 188).

In December 1969, the first oil reserves were found in the Norwegian sector of the North Sea. The oil industry grew rapidly and soon altered the composition of the country's business and industry to a considerable degree. In the coming decades, oil revenues would contribute to a profound transformation of the Norwegian economy.

From its modest start in the 1960s, immigration grew substantially. Up until about 1970, except for the Sami and Finnish minorities in the north and a tiny group of Roma people living mainly in Oslo, Norway was extremely homogenous and monocultural, with the main divide between urban and rural cultures being expressed most saliently in the conflicts connected with the language question. Over the past half-century, Norway has been transformed into a more multicultural and multilingual nation. This change is apparent in the larger cities especially, but features and problems associated with this new situation are clearly visible all over the country, and it is a frequent topic of discussion in the media.

The Sami people comprise the largest indigenous minority group. In 1992, Sami gained political recognition as an official language together with Norwegian in a number of municipalities in the northern part of the country.

Popular opinion was split on the question of joining the EC, later called the European Union. A referendum concerning Norwegian membership in 1972 resulted in a 54–46 per cent vote against joining, and this result was repeated in 1994, although the margin against membership was smaller (52–48 per cent). Both times, the processes and campaigns leading up to the vote engaged the population in political discussions to a degree which had rarely been seen in the usual biennial election campaigns. Citizen engagement with this issue before the 1972 referendum led to a change in the entire political climate of the country and contributed considerably to the radicalisation of society at large. This also had an important impact on the views and attitudes about both the language struggle and language planning in general.

The 1970s saw a growth in various popular movements throughout the country, the awakening of environmental awareness, and the establishment of a very active Marxist–Leninist Communist Party. The emerging feminist movement brought many women into the political arena, and in 1981 Gro Harlem Brundtland became Norway's first female Prime Minister. During her second government, in 1986, an important tradition began of attempting to have a close to complete gender balance in the Cabinet. Since then, any Norwegian government, regardless of its political persuasion, will follow this tradition and appoint at least 40 per cent female Cabinet ministers.

During the 1970s, a strong dialect movement had positive effects for the Nynorsk cause, and the long post-war decline of Nynorsk use in schools was finally halted. Radical Bokmål benefited significantly from the radical climate of the 1970s and became used more widely than ever before, especially among students and left-wing authors, and, in general, among supporters of more leftist political parties.

From the Language Peace Commission to the Language Council (1966–72)

The change of government in 1965 proved to have a deeper impact on the country's language policy than most people could anticipate. The Riksmål movement was very optimistic when the Labour government resigned in the autumn of 1965 and a coalition of non-socialist parties formed a new government. The leader of the Peasants' Party (which had now changed its name to the Centre Party) became Prime Minister. The largest party in the coalition, however, was the Conservative Party (*Høyre*) which throughout its history had been associated with support for the Riksmål movement and had as a consequence opposed the Labour Government's pan-Norwegian policy.

Riksmål supporters therefore had high expectations of seeing immediate consequences for language planning policy. When the Language Peace Commission published its report six months later, giving full support to most of the demands of the Riksmål movement, the situation looked very promising for a rapid victory for Riksmål.

What actually happened, however, turned out to be a total disappointment for the Riksmål movement. Even though the Conservative Party was the largest partner in the government coalition, the Cabinet member responsible for language and language planning policy was not from their party. The minister in charge, Kjell Bondevik (1901–83), Professor of Folklore at the University of Oslo, represented one of the smaller centrist parties, *Kristelig Folkeparti*, the Christian People's Party, which since its founding in the 1930s had strong ties to both the Nynorsk movement and pan-Norwegian aspirations. It was quite obvious that the new minister disagreed with many of the pro-Riksmål conclusions and recommendations of the Language

Peace Commission, and its recommendations were not implemented as quickly as could have been expected.

The radicalisation of Norwegian society following the political events of 1968 and the 1972 referendum played an important role in this. The campaign against EC membership mobilised people all over the country, involving many people who had previously been uninterested in politics. The establishment was firmly pro-membership, while the grass roots movement and all the rural areas as well as smaller towns were more or less united against it. When the 'No' side won, it was regarded as a seismic event in Norwegian society and politics, and this made a considerable impact on language policy as well.

The very concept of 'language peace' was soon questioned and problematised. Questions such as 'Language peace for whom?', 'On what basis?', 'Who will gain a sociolinguistic advantage by achieving language peace?' were put forth. Arguments from the pre-war period for a more class-oriented pan-Norwegian development reappeared in the discussions. This now led to a large number of young and politically active people viewing the language planning policies which had resulted in the reforms of 1917 and, in particular, of 1938, as part of a more general agenda with a clear democratic or socialist inclination. One obvious result of this was the increased use of Radical Bokmål.

Seen from this perspective, the 1959 Textbook Standard constituted a step backwards, and the Language Peace Commission was thus perceived as reactionary (cf. Wiggen 1973).

New arguments for Nynorsk

Towards the end of the 1960s and throughout the 1970s, the Nynorsk movement finally found alternative arguments to support their cause. New interest in Nynorsk as the standard of the peripheries, combined with a strong dialect movement, brought new young members and renewed optimism to the Nynorsk movement. A whole new generation of eager Nynorsk supporters surfaced – especially during the anti-EC campaign – and joined the youth organisation of Nynorsk activists (*Norsk målungdom*). The decline in the use of the Nynorsk standard in schools was halted in the mid-1970s. Alongside the political ideologies of 1968, insights provided by emerging branches of linguistics – sociolinguistics, the sociology of language, and language psychology – all inspired and stimulated the Nynorsk movement and provided it with effective new arguments for its cause.

Instead of the earlier strategy of concentrating on the issue of 'Norwegian' versus 'non-Norwegian' (or Danish) to recruit members into the Nynorsk movement, there was now a new understanding of how different varieties of spoken language function together in a community, how social provenance is reflected in language use, what it means to individuals to switch their language (even if only from one spoken variety of Norwegian to another), and how identity is inter-woven with a person's local dialect (Skirbekk et al. 1967; Furre 1968; Blakar 1973; Steinset and Kleiven 1975).

Analyses of the language situation from such new bases led many young people to conclude that the most frequently-used written Bokmål variety (Conservative Bokmål, which included the private Riksmål variety) represented society's upper classes and, in the rhetoric of the time, was thus the 'language of power'. In contrast, Nynorsk, being the written expression of the local dialects as well as the popular language spoken in both towns and rural areas, represented the oppo-site, as did Radical Bokmål. Sociolinguistically, the boundary was drawn between Nynorsk and Radical Bokmål on the one hand and Conservative Bokmål/Riksmål on the other.

Additionally, discussions about 'green' policies and the relationship between central and peripheral areas provided an important param-eter. The opposition between Bokmål and Nynorsk was well suited to the debate between the centre (Conservative Bokmål/Riksmål) and the periphery (Nynorsk). The defence of the peripheral areas of rural Norway included the defence of the dialects and of the Nynorsk standard. Support for Nynorsk was thus intimately connected with radical politics.

The Language Council (1972)

In its 1966 report, the Language Peace Commission recommended that the controversial Language Committee, with its 'restricted' mandate (that is, to work towards a pan-Norwegian solution on the basis of 'the people's language'), should be replaced by a language council. Parliament engaged in a lengthy debate about the language situation in 1970, based on a government White Paper published the year before. An act concerning the establishment of a language council was passed in 1971, and in 1972 the Language Council was established and began its work. It had forty-two members, comprising not only language experts and professionals (for example linguists, teachers and authors), as had been the case with the Language Committee, but also representatives of the three major groups involved in the language struggle: the Riksmål movement, the Nynorsk movement and the pan-Norwegian supporters. In addition, Parliament appointed eight of the members.

The Language Council's mandate was to develop policies that would lead to linguistic tolerance for all varieties of spoken and written Norwegian. The Riksmål movement rightfully regarded this mandate as an important victory, since it meant recognition for their own private written standard in addition to the official ones. However, the Language Council's mandate also stipulated that its subsidiary goal was to monitor the ongoing developments in spoken and written Norwegian and encourage tendencies that would in the long run contribute to bringing the written standards closer together.

However, this latter objective proved to have no impact whatsoever on the final results of the Council's language planning efforts. Immediately after the Council was established, it began preparations to reform Standard Bokmål, something the Language Peace Commission had particularly singled out as a necessary step in any appeasement process. However, by referring to the secondary aim in the Language Council's mandate, individuals who opposed the plan for official Bokmål to once again include the Riksmål forms deemed to be non-standard in 1938 were able to filibuster during the Council's deliberations. This reform process therefore took much longer to complete. The final result, however, could not be prevented: official Bokmål was changed in 1981 in the direction that the Riksmål movement had fought for in the late 1940s, 1950s and 1960s.

The 'Liberation Resolution' (1972)

In the meantime, immediately after the Language Council had been established it issued a resolution to placate the very impatient Riksmål movement, whose supporters resented the fact that it had taken six years since the Language Peace Commission's report for the Language Council to begin its work. This was due to a very detailed process of hearings followed by long deliberations in the Ministry of

Church and Education. In order to satisfy the most urgent demands of the Riksmål movement, the Council recommended what came to be called the 'Liberation Resolution' (*Liberaliseringsvedtaket*).

The implication of this resolution was that for three grammatical features, the use of non-standard upper-middle-class speech forms would not be corrected by teachers in pupils' essays written in Bokmål. The most important of these features concerned the definite article for nouns which were feminine in Standard Bokmål, since, as we saw earlier, the private Riksmål standard, as well as upper-middle-class speech, barely used the feminine grammatical gender, employing instead common (masculine/feminine) gender. The 1972 Resolution meant that if pupils wanted to, they could use the common gender system in their essays without penalty. This Resolution was announced through a letter sent out to schools in 1973 (*Norsk Skoleblad*, No. 25/1973).

The term the 'Liberation Resolution' is interesting. It showed that in the post-war period, the Riksmål movement – through its amazing level of activity, especially in the media – had managed to grasp the power to impose on the language struggle their own interpretations of the most important defining concepts: language freedom, pan-Norwegian, language liberation. They viewed this Resolution as 'liberating' people from, for example, having to adhere to the Bokmål standard's obligatory use of the feminine gender. This had been a focal point in the Riksmål movement's struggle against a pan-Norwegian policy. To many Riksmål supporters the use of the definite article -*a* for feminine nouns was seen as 'vulgar' and 'unnatural', emblematic of working-class and rural life. Therefore, the 'Liberation Resolution' meant that the children of Riksmål supporters were freed from having to use a form which to them was associated with the lower working classes. Of course, an alternative perspective would be that the introduction of obligatory feminine gender for about 900 nouns in the 1938 Bokmål standard constituted liberation for an overwhelming majority of Norwegians who consistently used the definite article -*a* for all feminine nouns when speaking.

The Bokmål reform of 1981

After the 'Liberation Resolution' was passed, preparations to move Standard Bokmål more in the direction of Riksmål progressed slowly.

In 1973, the Language Council appointed an *ad hoc* committee to instigate more reforms to Bokmål (Rambø 1999). This committee took much longer to complete its work than many Riksmål supporters anticipated. Their frustration was voiced in Parliament quite frequently by Members of Parliament who were Riksmål supporters. Time and again, the Riksmål organisations threatened to withdraw their representatives from the Language Council if their demands were not met immediately. The Language Council finally finished its deliberations in 1979, and a new set of reforms for Bokmål was passed by Parliament in 1981.

These reforms reintroduced a considerable number of upper-middle-class speech forms and features into standard written Bokmål. However, the way this was done made it possible once again to refer to the reform package as an act of 'liberation'. Many upper-middle-class speech forms which had been deemed non-standard in 1938 were labelled standard again. But only a few of the forms from working-class and southeastern dialects which had been part of Standard Bokmål since 1938 were removed from the standard, although in the ensuing years many more of these were dropped because they were used less frequently in printed texts. The 1981 reforms, however, merely added older Riksmål forms, which had the effect that Standard Bokmål after 1981 contained – for the individual writer – the possibility of even more variation than before. Everyone expected that the generally high social prestige of the Riksmål forms would ensure their frequent use, which is what happened, especially in school textbooks. Thus, Standard Bokmål in effect once again moved away from Standard Nynorsk.

The 1981 Bokmål reform was the first since 1910 that affected only one of the standards, and it was clearly anti-pan-Norwegian in nature. This represented the final proof that the post-war sociolinguistic counter-revolution had succeeded. It meant that the Riksmål movement now felt it could make certain concessions, and, in 1986, a minor but very important reform of the private Riksmål standard was implemented. Throughout the entire post-war period, many Riksmål supporters had shown their opposition to the pan-Norwegian policy by strongly championing certain important symbolic word forms that were cited over and over again. These included, among others:

nu 'now'
efter 'after'
sprog 'language'

whereas the Bokmål forms were:

nå (Nynorsk: *no*, but also *nå*)
etter (Nynorsk: *etter*)
språk (Nynorsk: *språk*)

In the heated debate of the 1950s and early 1960s, these Bokmål and Nynorsk standard forms were frowned upon by many Riksmål supporters as 'pan-Norwegian'. The Riksmål forms, which in the eyes of their supporters were the only possible versions, attained a symbolic value since they were so frequently used and showed the clear difference between Riksmål and 'pan-Norwegian'. However, these 'pan-Norwegian' forms were readily accepted into the private Riksmål standard as perfectly normal forms in the 1986 Riksmål reform. To many older Riksmål hardliners, who had battled over the course of several decades to keep the Riksmål forms and who maintained that the 'pan-Norwegian' forms would never be accepted into proper Riksmål, this change must have been difficult to accept. However, the 'pan-Norwegian' versions soon won out almost completely over the older Riksmål forms.

The end of a single-standard policy (2002)

From the Riksmål perspective, the Bokmål standard after the 1981 reforms still needed quite a lot of further alterations in order to rid it of the most obvious pan-Norwegian features. Therefore, throughout the 1980s and 1990s, the Language Council worked towards implementing yet another reform to Bokmål, which was issued finally in 2005. The fact that the 1981 and 2005 reforms both targeted only Bokmål, and a 2012 reform affected only Nynorsk, shows that a pan-Norwegian solution had been abandoned. The formal decision to terminate this approach was taken by Parliament in 2002. In light of the direction the Language Council's work had taken since 1972, it came as no surprise that a 2001 government White Paper recommended dropping the pan-Norwegian language planning policy, and

Parliament accepted this unanimously the following year. By doing so, politicians had diverged fundamentally from the main language planning goal espoused for almost a century.

Between 1910 and 1920, few people thought it possible that Norwegian society could elaborate and sustain two different written standards for Norwegian. By the turn of the millennium, most people realised that this was perfectly feasible. Over the years, many individuals had pointed to the fact that, throughout the nineteenth and twentieth centuries, literary and cultural works of high value had been created in both standards, and that if the nation was to lose either Bokmål or Nynorsk, this could not happen without serious damage to important national, literary and cultural values.

The 2005 Bokmål reform

While many upper-middle-class speech forms from the private Riksmål standard were reintroduced into Bokmål in 1981, the main thrust of the 2005 reform was to remove forms introduced during the pan-Norwegian period. At the same time, the hierarchical system from 1938 comprising main forms and minor/secondary forms was abolished, leaving only main forms in the standard. (For Nynorsk, the same was done in 2012.) This set of reforms removed from the Bokmål standard many working-class dialect elements as well as forms that were similar to those in Nynorsk; the motivation being that these 'lesser-used forms' rarely occurred in printed texts. But there was no apparent will on the part of the Riksmål movement to understand why these forms were used less frequently. Riksmål supporters were completely satisfied with the explanation that nobody wanted these pan-Norwegian forms, and therefore they were hardly ever seen in print. However, the strict censorship practiced by newspaper editors and publishing houses against all deviations from the most frequent word forms obviously played a role here. This linguistic censorship effectively prevented elements from Radical Bokmål being used in private enterprise publications, leaving very limited opportunities for these forms to appear at all.

One example of this is described in Jahr (2010). It concerns the eastern rural and working-class dialect 'double infinitive' (with some infinitives ending in -e, others in -a), which was removed from the Bokmål standard in the 2005 reform. This feature of the eastern dialects was labelled a minor form (*sideform*) in Bokmål in 1938, but it had been accepted in essays written by school pupils since 1919. However, this feature was rarely found in print. Very few individuals were aware that it was allowed in the official standard. It is also probable that even if people knew this, most of them would hesitate to use it, preferring to stay with the traditional -*e* ending. But the few who both knew that the double infinitive was officially allowed in Bokmål *and* wanted to use it in their writing were effectively stopped from doing so through the linguistic censorship exerted by newspapers and publishing houses. On the Internet, however, where people can write freely without being corrected, the more frequent use of the double infinitive (Jahr 2010: 134) shows that a 'lesser used' status of this linguistic feature is problematic.

The Riksmål movement saw no problem in this practice of private censorship. Indeed, Riksmål supporters interpreted this as 'free language development' (*fri sprogutvikling*), as opposed to the official language planning policy determined by Parliament and the government, which they often described as almost a misuse of state power ('*den statlige sprogtvang*').

The removal from Bokmål of many of the forms branded by Riksmål supporters as 'pan-Norwegian' was, to most people, of no great concern. They had never been told in school or anywhere else that their oral language forms had been included in official Standard Bokmål since 1938, and so they had never considered using them in writing.

The 'language planning by voting' system (1972–2002)

It is interesting to note that the 1981 and 2005 reforms were not totally consistent with the principles laid out in the Language Peace Commission's 1966 report. In 1981, not all former Riksmål forms were reintroduced into the standard; and in 2005, a few forms from working-class dialects were allowed which differed from the parallel Nynorsk forms. Since these new items could not be labelled 'pan-Norwegian' elements, it proved easier for Riksmål supporters to accept them. These forms consisted of past tense verbs in -*øy*- where Nynorsk had -*au*-: *brøyt* ('broke'), *røyk* ('smoked, streamed'), *skøyt* ('shot') and so on, instead of *braut*, *rauk*, *skaut*. The forms with -*au*- were simultaneously removed from the Bokmål standard as being 'lesser-used forms'.

One reason for this inconsistency was the Language Council's practice of 'language planning by voting' (Jahr 1996). All important decisions about reinstating forms in Bokmål had to be supported by a majority of the twenty-one Bokmål representatives on the Council. During the 1970s, most of the decisions to reinstate Riksmål forms were passed with only a slight margin, while the forms that failed to be accepted always were rejected by a very slight margin.

Since 2005, even though many individual so-called pan-Norwegian forms had been removed from the Bokmål standard, the basic systematic features of Radical Bokmål were nevertheless kept intact: the feminine gender option (with the postposed definite article -a), and the past-tense ending -a for weak verbs of the 1st conjugation. The Bokmål standard now provides the individual writer with the option of using the feminine gender or of marking only some nouns as feminine. This seemingly full grammatical freedom regarding grammatical gender is, however, seriously restricted by the still quite rigorous censorship carried out by many newspapers, magazines and publishing houses. Only famous authors of fiction such as Per Petterson (b. 1952) are allowed to use the Radical Bokmål variety without being 'corrected' by newspapers or publishing houses. All other writers, including university professors of Norwegian, are 'corrected' if they use Standard Bokmål forms which deviate from the parallel forms preferred by the print media. These changes are carried out under the pretext that newspapers always have to correct orthographic errors occurring in letters to the editor or submitted articles. Jahr (2005) discusses instances of this type of correction made by one of the major publishing houses in Oslo.

The 2012 Nynorsk reform

During the 1980s the Language Council made several minor changes to Nynorsk which indicated a departure from the earlier policy of a pan-Norwegian strategy. And like the reforms to Bokmål in 1981 and 2005, the 2012 Nynorsk reforms were not carried out from a pan-Norwegian perspective, but were focused solely on Nynorsk and Nynorsk users, with no consideration whatever of the Bokmål standard. The clear tendency permeating this reform was a consolidation of what can be termed mainstream Nynorsk usage over the past thirty to fifty years. This means that, as was the case with changes to Bokmål in

2005, forms which had been less visible in print were removed from the Nynorsk standard. The reform committee's mandate was to make a substantial reduction in parallel forms which provided the individual writer with options. The result was a reduction in optional forms indeed, but perhaps not to the degree to which many individuals had wished.

Summary: defeat for the pan-Norwegian policy?

The textbook standard of 1959 outwardly signalled that the pan-Norwegian policy would continue. In reality, however, the planned development towards a pan-Norwegian standard based on 'the people's language' was quickly losing ground, as events occurred behind the scenes. Most important was the fact that the Labour Party leaders wanted to get out of their commitment to a pan-Norwegian policy. The language question was in effect the only issue on which the political opposition could effectively attack the Labour Government, which held a clear majority in Parliament throughout the 1950s. And without active support from the Labour Party, the 1938 reforms proved difficult to defend.

In the 2001 White Paper, the non-socialist government then in power declared that the pan-Norwegian policy had proved to be a failure and that it was no longer going to be pursued politically. When a resolution to this effect was passed by Parliament in 2002, the Riksmål movement, which had been much weakened partly as a result of its success with the 1981 reforms, gained a victory which its supporters in the 1950s could only have dreamt of. None the less, it was the work carried out in the 1950s and early 1960s that finally brought about the outcome they wanted. In the long run, the experiment of introducing linguistic elements 'from below' into Bokmål did not achieve the necessary political and public support it required.

The post-war sociolinguistic counter-revolution happened in three phases: while the first one was basically political, the following two were dominated by language planning. The political phase comprised the struggle of the late 1940s, 1950s and 1960s to win the support of the general public and force the politicians to change the course of language planning policy away from the pan-Norwegian goal. The language planning phase covered the period 1972–2012, which saw two reforms to Bokmål (1981 and 2005) and one to Nynorsk (2012) signalling important milestones.

Does this mean that the pan-Norwegian policy was a failure from the very start, and that the whole idea of aiming for a single written standard was proved wrong by the developments of the twentieth century? The answer to this question depends on the perspective we choose to take.

The Riksmål movement, as well as most of the Nynorsk support-ers, probably feel that the pan-Norwegian policy was a complete failure. This is certainly the view of most politicians today and that of the interested general public. Others, however, point to the fact that some of the most symbolic Riksmål word forms from the struggle during the 1950s and 1960s have now been replaced – in the Riksmål standard – by formerly frowned-upon 'pan-Norwegian' forms, and these symbolic Riksmål elements now appear to be more and more outdated. On the basis of this fact, which involves only a few – albeit frequently used – words, some people have claimed a victory for pan-Norwegian. It is true that the fight in the 1950s was very much focused on these word forms, and the now accepted versions (*nå, etter, språk, snø*) were all branded by the Riksmål supporters at the time as being totally unacceptable. Still, claiming victory for pan-Norwegian – even using the post-war Riksmål definition of 'pan-Norwegian' that more or less equates it with Radical Bokmål – is without any founda-tion. The pan-Norwegian policy aimed for a single written standard. The current situation is far from this reality, even though the two official standards are closer together now linguistically than they were one hundred years ago.

On the other hand, with regard to the question of whether or not the pan-Norwegian policy has proven to be a mistake, it is interesting to observe that in 2002, when Parliament formally abandoned the pan-Norwegian policy, nobody made a serious point of the extra expense involved in the decision to sustain two official national language stand-ards. Early in the twentieth century, the financial argument for saving money for both the government and society at large was decisive; in 2002 the country had become so prosperous that the extra costs of maintaining and sustaining two national standards were no obstacle, so it was easy for Parliament unanimously to end this controversial language planning policy. The main change was the political accept-ance of the permanent use of two official national standards.

The economic motivation for a pan-Norwegian language planning policy, deemed absolutely necessary early in the twentieth century, has over the course of time led to many interesting processes, debates, fights and decisions, all of which help students of language planning to gain valuable insights into various aspects of language planning activities and opportunities – first and foremost into how language planning in Norway became part of a unique sociolinguistic experiment.

CHAPTER 9

Summary and concluding remarks

This book started out with some essential questions concerning the limits of language planning. How far can language planning go? Is it possible to change the sociolinguistic landscape of an entire language community – a country for instance?

We have now reached the end of our journey through the history of language planning and language struggles in modern Norway. In Norway itself, at the time of writing (2013) the sea is calm where earlier it was very rough. The 'linguistic avalanche' which Einar Haugen (1966a) said was still sliding has finally come to a halt. So what are the results of a century-and-a-half of language planning and linguistic strife?

Major conclusions

Two major conclusions can be drawn from the history of language planning policies in modern Norway:

1. It is possible to achieve far-reaching results if language planning – involving corpus as well as status planning – is consistent with the dominant contemporary ideology. This happened during the period between 1814 and 1917, when language planning was conducted primarily within a nationalist framework.
2. If language planning involves crossing important sociolinguistic boundaries in a given society, it will need extensive backing and support from a powerful political movement in order to succeed.

Such action must be an inherent part of the movement's ideology and programme. From 1917 to 1966, during the sociopolitical period in Norway, language planning policy of this type was attempted, but did not succeed.

Seen from a language planning perspective, the first Norwegian period must be viewed as successful in most respects. The main aim was to develop a national standard which differed from the other Scandinavian languages. By 1917, the country had developed not one but two national standards, both of which were clearly distinguishable from Danish and Swedish. The main problem facing language planners during the second, sociopolitical, period was how to overcome the problem created during the nationalist period: the existence of two standards which were constantly competing with each other. In the decade 1910–1920, very few people thought it would be possible for the country to maintain two national standards.

Parliament's solution was to undertake a language planning programme that would steer the two standards towards a merger into a single pan-Norwegian (*samnorsk*) standard. The hope underlying this plan was that, if successful, it would solve the language question for good and end the language conflict: the country would end up with one national standard only. Linguistically, the two standards were close and thus completely mutually intelligible. Sociolinguistically, however, they differed substantially. This soon proved to be the main challenge for merging the two standards into a single alternative. At the time, the language planners in general did not comprehend the sociolinguistic problems that lay ahead. And supporters of each of the two standards claimed that their standard was the only one which was suitable for the whole country.

The politically-radical language planning aim of the 1930s, and the means employed to achieve it, represented a unique sociolinguistic experiment which had not been seen anywhere else. If successful, this policy would have resulted in a sociolinguistic revolution, establishing the spoken varieties of the lower classes – workers and peasants – as the norm for the nation's only written standard. Elevating lower-class speech to such a role could only occur at the expense of the upper-middle-class spoken variety. However, even though in the 1930s the Labour Party accepted Professor Halvdan Koht's analysis of the linguistic situation and followed it up with political action in 1938, not everyone in the Party was wholeheartedly behind the policy. And as opposition to the pan-Norwegian policy grew stronger in the 1950s, scepticism about it within the Labour Party increased. The Party's pre-war ideological arguments for promoting the 'people's language' gave way to a typically pragmatic motivation: it was uneconomical and impractical for a small nation to maintain two linguistically very similar national standards.

This line of argument was clearly inadequate for defending such a politically-radical sociolinguistic programme. A consistent policy would have required new reforms to be instituted in order to build on what had begun in 1917 and 1938. This, however, never happened. Instead, the appointment of the Language Peace Commission in 1964 signalled that the sociolinguistic experiment had in reality been abandoned. Without backing from the Labour Party, such a daring policy could not withstand the impressive amount of resistance mobilised by the opponents of this official language planning policy (cf. Bull 1993).

Therefore, from the standpoint of the expressed intentions of Parliament to create a single standard out of two, the second period of language planning cannot be regarded as successful. The means employed to develop such a standard proved too difficult to implement due to broad opposition and resistance from the large number of people and important groups in society who used the written language the most. The single-standard policy, a goal taken for granted by nearly everyone until far into the twentieth century, was therefore finally dropped by the political authorities, and a permanent two-standard situation was readily accepted by Parliament in 2002, after a long transition period from 1966.

Lessons of the pan-Norwegian policy

The fate of the pan-Norwegian policy (cf. Jahr 1997a) is an illustration of the difficulties which language planning will inevitably encounter if changes to the standard are perceived by influential groups in society as unacceptable for sociolinguistic reasons. The outcome for the pan-Norwegian policy strongly suggests that a sociolinguistically-radical language planning policy can only be implemented successfully if it is backed up by a strong political movement whose members agree about the analysis, who support its methods, and who look forward to achieving its aims. Exclusively practical arguments in favour of changes that involve crossing salient sociolinguistic boundaries appear to be inadequate for achieving this.

The 1938 language reform stands as a daring attempt at changing the sociolinguistic pattern of an entire country. With respect to the written standard, the experiment failed, mainly due to long and successful civil resistance and to decreasing support from the Labour Party. There was no grass-roots movement behind the pan-Norwegian policy. In contrast, since the nineteenth century, the Landsmål/Nynorsk cause has always been backed by a large grass-roots movement, as well as by political parties and other groups.

Nynorsk – the current situation

It took the Nynorsk movement several decades to recuperate after World War II, and in the meantime internal conflicts took their toll on its members and the entire movement. In the radical atmosphere of the 1970s, the situation finally changed for the better for the Nynorsk cause. Its decline in schools stopped at around 16.5 per cent and stayed at that level for several years. However, when in the late 1980s and 1990s the language struggle more or less vanished as a central political issue, the decline of Nynorsk in the schools continued. As of 2013, 12 per cent to 13 per cent of school children use Nynorsk as their main written standard, and around 10 per cent of the total population report that they use it. However, in large areas of the western part of the country, Nynorsk still dominates.

In spite of the fact that Nynorsk is used by a rather small minority, the standard is firmly protected by law. A special Language Act was passed by Parliament, first in 1930 (Bruheim 1982; Grønvik 1987) and again in 1980, ensuring the rights of individual Bokmål and Nynorsk users. The law also asserts that the two standards have equal official status. This renders the legal position and protection of Nynorsk as the minority standard stronger today that it ever was before World War II, which subsequently ensures the use of Nynorsk by the authorities, in schools as well as on radio and television. Nynorsk appears less often in daily newspapers, magazines and private enterprise. However, in recent decades some newspapers have started to include more Nynorsk. The Oslo daily *Klassekampen* is perhaps the best example of this, but other newspapers also now print more articles in Nynorsk than before. In the Norwegian Lutheran Church, Nynorsk has a secure standing, since quite a number of congregations have opted for it. Several of Norway's leading contemporary authors are Nynorsk users. Therefore, Nynorsk has a much stronger representation in literary fiction than in society at large, being used by prominent authors such as Edvard Hoem (b. 1949), novelist Kjartan Fløgstad (b. 1944) and playwright Jon Fosse (b. 1959), among others.

Many Bokmål users resent the fact that schoolchildren are obliged to learn Nynorsk at school when their main standard is Bokmål. These children have no use for Nynorsk, the claim goes. Politically, it is quite controversial that Nynorsk is compulsorily taught in the schools to everybody. The Conservative Party (*Høyre*) still wants to abolish the obligatory Nynorsk essay for the high-school exam, a position the party has held for more than a century. Whether they will succeed or not in the near future remains to be seen, but Nynorsk supporters fear that the position of Nynorsk as a national standard would in effect be lost should this compulsory Nynorsk exam essay be dropped.

While the Nynorsk organisation *Noregs Mållag* remains strong and vibrant, *Riksmålsforbundet* is a small and rather insignificant association. The same is true of *Landslaget for språklig samling*, the group which is still pushing for a pan-Norwegian standard, despite the official state policy to drop this aspiration in 2002. This tiny pan-Norwegian organisation, however, never had the strong public backing which *Riksmålsforbundet* previously enjoyed, and which *Noregs Mållag* still does.

Bokmål – the current situation

Bokmål, formerly Riksmål, has always been the majority standard. Its origin and history make it unique as a national standard. While Nynorsk has close or quite similar European parallels (for example, Faroese, and Macedonian), no known national standard has a history and development like Bokmål's.

We have seen that Danish was the starting point for this variety and that it underwent changes through several minor and major reforms. At first, upper-middle-class speech – the Dano-Norwegian creoloid – functioned as the obvious norm for the changes; then we saw how the norm base shifted to the 'people's language' during the phase of the pan-Norwegian policy. After a long period of conflict, the pendulum swung back again. Moderate Bokmål is currently the most unmarked and by far the most frequently used form of Bokmål, with its other varieties being sidelined and considered clearly more marked. The censorship exerted by many newspaper editors and publishing houses is still very effective, and also contributes to the situation where only one Bokmål variety dominates. Some authors of fiction, however, use more radical varieties of Bokmål which are closer to the local south-eastern working-class and rural dialects; Per Petterson (cf. p. 160) is the most prominent of the authors who write in Radical Bokmål.

The most unmarked Bokmål variety today makes more use of the common gender (with the definite ending *-en*) than before 1981, the year of the Bokmål reform which made the use of the feminine gender optional. However, some frequently used words have been retained in their 1938 versions, and these words often became the focus of attention during the 1950s and 1960s, being branded 'pan-Norwegian' by the Riksmål supporters: *etter* 'after' (vs. *efter*), *nå* 'now' (vs. *nu*), *språk* 'language' (vs. *sprog*) – all three were formally accepted into the private Riksmål standard in 1986 – as well as *farge* 'colour' (vs. *farve*), *fram* 'forward' (vs. *frem*, although *frem* is now used quite frequently after having been brought back into the Bokmål standard in 2005), and others.

Dialect maintenance today

The year 1924 bore witness to the last serious dispute concerning the use of local dialects, both rural and urban, in schools. Since then, most people have accepted the ruling that pupils can use their own local dialects in school. Teachers should also use the local dialect if that feels natural to them, or at least adjust their spoken language as much as possible towards the dialect of their pupils. The same principle is laid out in the current Norwegian School Act:

> For oral language in the classroom, pupils and teaching staff decide for themselves which spoken variety [of Norwegian] they will use. The teaching staff and school managers, in their own choice of vocabulary and expressions, shall also take into consideration as much as possible the spoken variety [that is, the local dialect] of the pupils. (Jahr 2008: 157; author's translation.)

This principle has proved to be of paramount importance for dialect maintenance in Norway. It has effectively prevented any spoken variety from becoming a generally accepted standard in society at large or a subject in the school curriculum (Venås 1992b; Jahr 1997b, 2008). Instead, considerable linguistic knowledge of the different local dialects in the country is required of high-school students. The fact that today Norway stands out as probably the country in Europe which uses local dialects the most – with an official ideology that the situation should be kept that way – is basically the result of this principle, which was first formulated by Parliament in 1878. A decade ago, Peter Trudgill summed up the Norwegian situation in this way: 'Norway is also one of the most dialect-speaking countries in Europe . . . there is an enormous social tolerance for linguistic diversity' (2002: 31).

This social tolerance for linguistic diversity ties in with a specific sociolinguistic consequence of the 1938 reforms: the demotion of upper-middle-class speech as a model for other speakers, and the subsequent upgrading and increasing acceptance of dialect use. Between the two World Wars, upper-middle-class speech was considered by most people – excluding Nynorsk users and its supporters, obviously – as the only serious linguistic target for an oral standard. It represented a high-status variety which also mirrored the most frequently used version of standard written Riksmål. Today, however, very few people, if any, would look to that particular spoken variety as a model for their own speech. Since the 1970s, most people who for whatever reason want to change their spoken dialect usually look to written Bokmål as their target with reference to word forms and morphology. This involves, for example, more use of the feminine gender ending –a, as well as word forms such as beit 'bit' (pret.), feit 'fat' (adj.), hage 'garden', mage 'belly, stomach', røyk 'smoke', stein 'stone', sør 'south', snø 'snow', vitenskap 'science', and so on, than in traditional upper-middle-class speech (which has bet, fet, have, mave, røk, sten, syd, sne, videnskap, and so on). From being accepted more or less by a majority of the population as standard spoken Norwegian – Nynorsk users and supporters again excluded – upper-middle-class speech has over the past decades come to be perceived as just one of the many spoken varieties of Norwegian, albeit one of the more prestigious. It is no longer viewed by society at large as a neutral, unmarked oral standard variety, as was previously the case.

The 1938 reforms therefore appear to have had a sociolinguistic impact on spoken Norwegian. The experiment of introducing lower-status forms into Bokmål has had, it seems, a lasting social effect on the oral upper-middle-class variety, putting it more on a par socio-linguistically with urban and rural dialects around the country. This ties in with the principle of oral instruction in schools, and with the widespread dialect use that is taken for granted in all social groups and domains in Norway, including radio and television.

Two national standards continue – Norway will still be special

The situation of maintaining two written Norwegian national standards will most probably continue long into the foreseeable future. Linguistically, the two standards are more similar today than they were before the pan-Norwegian policy was being pursued, but socio-linguistically they are still clearly different. This divergence harks back to the two opposing social bases on which Ivar Aasen and Knud Knudsen founded their language planning policies in the nineteenth century. Today, the differences between these two social bases are still salient, although, as we have just seen, the status of upper-middle-class speech has been reduced considerably compared to what it was prior to the 1938 reforms.

Since Einar Haugen published his pioneering monograph about Norwegian language planning and language conflict in 1966, the language situation in modern Norway has become a celebrated case in the international language planning literature. Earlier accounts of the development of Norwegian, however, have often focused more on corpus planning technicalities: the many and significant changes in orthography and morphology, and changes carried out to thousands of individual words in the various language reforms of the nineteenth and twentieth centuries. There are obviously notable exceptions to this (Vikør 1975 being a good example), and Haugen himself (1966a) gives much more of a political and social context to the various reforms than many other accounts. Nevertheless, neither Haugen nor most other descriptions of the Norwegian case have focused primarily, as we have done in this book, on the fundamental processes that have shaped the complex sociopolitical environment in which language planning has been conducted in modern Norway.

Such a perspective has provided an opportunity to suggest a coherent explanation of the driving forces behind the developments and conflicting language planning positions which have shaped the modern Norwegian language situation.

References

(Note: Christiania = Kristiania = Oslo)

Aars, Jacob Jonathan (1885), *Retskrivnings-Regler til Skolebrug* [*Orthographic rules for use in schools*], 7th edition, Kristiania: Fabritius.

Aars, Jacob Jonathan, Simon Wright Hofgaard and Moltke Moe (1898), *Om en del retskrivnings- og sprogspørsmaal. Redegjørelse til det kongelige departement for kirke- og undervisningsvæsenet* [*On some orthographic and language questions. Report to the Royal Ministry of Church and Education*] (= Universitets- og skole-annaler 13, Bilag 1), Kristiania: A. W. Brøgger.

Aasen, Ivar [1836] (1909), 'Om vort skriftsprog' ['On our written language'], *Syn og Segn*, pp. 1–5.

Aasen, Ivar (1848), *Det norske Folkesprogs Grammatik* [*Grammar of the Norwegian people's language*], Kristiania: Werner & Comp.

Aasen, Ivar (1850), *Ordbog over det norske Folkesprog* [*Dictionary of the Norwegian people's language*], Kristiania: Werner & Comp.

Aasen, Ivar (1853), *Prøver af Landsmaalet i Norge* [*Samples of the Landsmaal in Norway*], Christiania: Werner & Comp.

Aasen, Ivar (1855), *Ervingen. Sangspil i een Akt* [*The heir. Singspiel in one scene*], Christiania: Det Norske Theaters Forlag.

Aasen, Ivar (1863), *Symra. Tvo Tylvter med nya Visor* [*Symra. Two dozen new songs*], Christiania: Malling. (Final edition 1875.)

Aasen, Ivar (1864), *Norsk Grammatik* [*Norwegian Grammar*], Christiania: Malling.

Aasen, Ivar (1873), *Norsk Ordbog* [*Norwegian Dictionary*], Christiania: Malling.

Aasen, Ivar (1875), *Heimsyn – Ei snøgg Umsjaaing yver Skapningen og Menneskja, tilmaatad fyre Ungdomen* [*A view of the world. A quick look at the creation and man, tailored for the youth*], Kristiania: Det Norske Samlaget.

Aftenposten, 3 May 1946. Oslo.

Almenningen, Olaf, Arve Elvik, Bottolv Helleland, Åsmund Lien and Lars S. Vikør (eds) (1981), *Målreising i 75 år. Noregs Mållag 1906–1981* [*75 years of language uprising. Noregs Mållag 1906–1981*], Oslo: Fonna.

Andersen, Elsa Stenby (1977), *En studie i første-utgaven av Rolfsens leseverk, med særlig vekt på gjengivelse og normering av skjønnlitterære tekster* [*A study of the first edition of Rolfsen's reader with special emphasis on reproduction and normalisation of non-fiction texts*], unpublished Cand. Philol. thesis, University of Oslo, Department of Scandinavian Studies.

Baldauf, Richard B. Jr and Rober B. Kaplan (eds) (2006), *Language planning and policy in Europe, Vol. 2: The Czech Republic, the European Union and Northern Ireland*, Clevedon-Buffalo-Toronto: Multilingual Matters Ltd.

Berg, Thoralf (1977), *Debatten om et norsk scenespråk i Christiania 1848–1853 med hovedvekt på Knud Knudsen og hans arbeid for et norsk scenespråk ved Den norske dramatiske Skoles Theater i sesongene 1852/53* [*The debate about a Norwegian stage idiom in Oslo 1848–1853 with the main emphasis on Knud Knudsen and his work for a Norwegian language on stage at The Norwegian dramatic school's theatre in the seasons 1852/53*], unpublished Cand. Philol. thesis, University of Trondheim, Department of Scandinavian Studies.

Bernsen, Marit (1975), *Den 'sosiale' argumentasjon for målsak blant målstudenter i tiden 1923–1938 og dens forutsetninger* [*The 'social' argument for the Nynorsk cause among the Nynorsk student supporters during the period 1923–1938, and its background*], unpublished Cand. Philol. thesis, University of Bergen, Department of Scandinavian Studies.

Bjerke, André (1960), *Ti års kamp for riksmålet* [*Ten years' of struggle for Riksmål*], Oslo: Riksmålsforbundet.

Bjerke, André [1963] (1968), 'Brennstoff til et bokbål' ['Books as fuel for a bonfire'], in A. Bjerke, *Hårdt mot hårdt*, Oslo: Riksmålsforbundet, pp. 81–9.

Bjørklund, Oddvar (1970), *Marcus Thrane. Sosialistleder i et u-land* [*Marcus Thrane. Socialist leader in a developing country*], Oslo: Tiden.

Blakar, Rolf (1973), *Språk er makt* [*Language is power*], Oslo: Pax.

Bleken, Brynjulv (1956), *Studier i Knud Knudsens grammatiske arbeider* [*Studies in Knud Knudsen's grammatical works*], Bidrag til nordisk filologi av studerende ved Universitetet i Oslo, Oslo: I Kommisjon hos Aschehoug & Co.

Bleken, Brynjulv (1966), *Om norsk sprogstrid* [*On the Norwegian language struggle*] (= Skrifter utgitt av Det Norske Akademi for Sprog og Litteratur 4), Oslo: Universitetsforlaget.

Blix, Elias (1869), *Nokre Salmar, gamle og nye* [*Some hymns, old and new*], Christiania: Det Norske Samlaget.

Bruheim, Magnhild (1982), *Mållova frå 1930. Bakgrunn, gjennomføring og oppfølging den fyrste tida* [*The Language Act of 1930: Background, implementation and follow-up in the initial period*], unpublished Cand. Philol. thesis, University of Oslo, Department of Scandinavian Studies.

Bucken-Knapp, Gregg (2003), *Elites, language, and the politics of identity: the Norwegian case in comparative perspective*, Albany, NY: State University of New York Press.

Bull, Tove (1987), '1885 enda ein gong' ['1885 once again'], *Maal og Minne*, pp. 98–136.

Bull, Tove (1993), 'Conflicting ideologies in contemporary Norwegian language planning', in E.H. Jahr (ed.), *Language conflict and language planning* (= Trends in Linguistics. Studies and Monographs 72), Berlin/New York: Mouton de Gruyter, pp. 21–37.

Bull, Tove (2002), 'Elias Blix og framveksten av det nynorske kyrkjespråket' ['Elias Blix and the development of Nynorsk as an ecclesiastical language'], *Språknytt* 30.1, pp. 9–11.

Bull, Trygve (1980), *For å si det som det var –* [*To say it as it was –*], Oslo: Cappelen.

Burgun, Achille (1919), *Le développement linguistique en Norvège depuis 1814* [*Linguistic development in Norway after 1814*], 1re partie (= Videnskapsselskapets Skrifter II, Hist.-Filos. Klasse, 1917, No. 1), Kristiania: I Kommission hos Jacob Dybwad.

Burgun, Achille (1921), *Le développement linguistique en Norvège depuis 1814* [*Linguistic development in Norway after 1814*], IIe partie (= Videnskapsselskapets Skrifter II, Hist.-Filos. Klasse, 1919, No. 5), Kristiania: En Commission chez Jacob Dybwad.

Christensen, Henrik Melgaard (2009), *På norsk folkemåls grunn. Arbeiderpartiets språkpolitikk fra 1929 til 1990* [*On the basis of the people's language. The Labour Party's language policy from 1929 to 1990*], unpublished MA thesis, University of Oslo, Department of Archaeology, Conservation and History.

Cooper, Robert L. (1989), *Language planning and social change*, Cambridge: Cambridge University Press.

Dahl, Hans Fredrik (1975), *Hallo – hallo! Kringkastingen i Norge 1920–1940* [*Hello – hello! Radio broadcasting in Norway 1920–1940*], Oslo: Cappelen.

Dahl, Helge (1962), *Knud Knudsen og latinskolen* [*Knud Knudsen and the Latin school*], Oslo: Universitetsforlaget.

Dal, Ingerid (1963a), 'Forfinelse og nyanserikdom – eller oppløsningssymptomer?' ['Refinement and richness of nuances – or symptoms of disintegration?'], *Frisprog* 21 September, Oslo.

Dal, Ingerid (1963b), 'Respekt for kjensgjerninger' ['Respect for facts'], *Morgenbladet* 9 October, Oslo.

Dale, Johs. A. (1950), *Studiar i Arne Garborgs språk og stil* [*Studies of Arne Garborg's language and style*], Oslo: Aschehoug.

Den nye rettskrivning (1917a), *Den nye rettskrivning. Regler og ordlister utarbeidet ved Den departementale rettskrivningskomite. I Riksmål* [*The new orthography. Rules and word lists prepared by the Ministry's orthography committee. I Riksmål*], Kristiania: Det Mallingske Bogtrykkeri 1918.

Den nye rettskrivning (1917b), *Den nye rettskrivning. Reglar og ordlistor utarbeidde ved Den departementale rettskrivningskomite. II Landsmål* [*The new orthography. Rules and word lists prepared by the Ministry's orthography committee. II For Landsmål*], Kristiania: Det Mallingske Bogtrykkeri 1918.

Det Norske Arbeiderparti (1933), *Sprog- og andre kulturspørsmål* [*Language and other cultural issues*], Oslo: Det Norske Arbeiderparti.

Eitrem, Hans, Amund B. Larsen and Steinar Schjøtt (1909), *Utredning av spørsmaalet om et mulig samarbeide mellem landsmaal og riksmaal i retskrivningen* [*Inquiry into the question of a possible cooperation between Landsmaal and Riksmaal in orthography*], Tillæg 3 til

Universitets- og Skole-annaler for 1909, Kristiania: Kirke- og Undervisningsdepartementet.

Elmevik, Lennart and Ernst Håkon Jahr (eds) (2012), *Contact between Low German and Scandinavian in the Late Middle Ages. 25 years of research* (= Acta Academiae Regiae Gustavi Adolphi 121), Uppsala: Kungl. Gustav Adolfs Akademien för svensk folkkultur.

Elswijk, Roald J. J. H. van (2010), 'Spread the word. Arne and Hulda Garborg as cultural transmitters of Nynorsk', in P. Broomans and M. Ronne (eds), *In the vanguard of cultural transfer. Cultural transmitters and authors in peripheral literary fields* (= Studies on cultural transfer & transmission 2), Groningen: Barkhuis, pp. 13–31.

Falk, Hjalmar (1900), 'De haarde Konsonanter' ['The hard consonants'], *Aftenposten* 8 May, No. 338, Kristiania.

Falnes, Oscar J. (1933), *National romanticism in Norway* (= Columbia University Studies in history, economics and public law 386), New York: Columbia University Press.

Fishman, Joshua A. (1997), *In praise of the beloved language. A comparative view of positive ethnolinguistic consciousness* (= Contributions to the sociology of language 76), Berlin/New York: Mouton de Gruyter.

Fløgstad, Kjartan (2004), *Brennbart [Inflammable]*, Oslo: Gyldendal.

Framlegg (1966), *Framlegg til samlenormal [Recommendation for a Pan-Norwegian standard]* (= Språklig Samlings Småskrifter 1), Oslo: Landslaget for Språklig Samling.

Furre, Berge (ed.) (1968), *Målreising 1967. Eit debattopplegg. Tilråding frå ei målpolitisk programnemnd i Noregs Mållag [Language struggle 1967. A programme for debate. Recommendations from the language-political programme committee of Noregs Mållag]*, Oslo: Det Norske Samlaget.

Furre, Berge (1997), 'Då nynorsk vart kyrkjemål' ['When Nynorsk became a church language'], *Syn og Segn*, pp. 20–6.

Garborg, Arne (1877), *Den ny-norske Sprog- og Nationalitetsbevægelse: Et Forsøg paa en omfattende Redegjørelse, formet som polemiske sendebreve til Modstræverne [The Nynorsk linguistic and national movement: an attempt at a comprehensive account, written as polemical letters to its adversaries]*, Kristiania: I kommision hos Alb. Cammermeyer.

Garborg, Arne (1918), *Homer: Odyssevskvædet. Paa norskt ved Arne Garborg [Homer: The Odyssey. In Norwegian by Arne Garborg]*, Kristiania: Aschehoug.

Gerdener, Wilhelm (1986), *Der Purismus im Nynorsk: historische Entwicklung und heutiger Sprachgebrauch* [*Purism in Nynorsk: historic development and current use*] (= Münstersche Beiträge zur deutschen und nordischen Philologie 1), Münster: Kleinheinrich.

Grepstad, Ottar (2013), *Historia om Ivar Aasen* [*The History of Ivar Aasen*], Oslo: Det Norske Samlaget.

Grønvik, Oddrun (1987), *Målbruken i offentleg teneste i tida 1930–1940* [*Government language use in the period 1930–1940*], Oslo: Det Norske Samlaget.

Gundersen, Dag (1967), *Fra Wergeland til Vogt-komiteen: et utvalg av hovedtrekk og detaljer fra norsk språknormering* [*From Wergeland to the Vogt committee: a selection of chief developments and details from Norwegian language planning*], Oslo: Universitetsforlaget.

Guttu, Tor (2007), 'Foreldreaksjonen 1949–1954 – den største folkebevegelse inntil da' ['The Parents' Action 1949–1954 – the biggest popular movement up till then'], *Språknytt* 35.3, pp. 1–4.

Haaland, Øyvind (1980), *Riksmålsmann, landsmålsmann og nordmann. En presentasjon av Moltke Moes språksyn og plass i norsk språkhistorie* [*Riksmål supporter, Nynorsk supporter, and Norwegian. An account of Moltke Moe's linguistics views and place in Norwegian language history*], unpublished Cand. Philol. thesis, University of Oslo, Department of Scandinavian Studies.

Hægstad, Marius, Arne Garborg and Rasmus Flo (1899), *Framlegg til skrivereglar for landsmaale i skularne* [*Recommendations for rules for Landsmaal in the schools*] (= Tillæg til universitets- og skoleannaler), Kristiania: A. W. Brøggers Bogtrykkeri. Cf. also (1901), *Tillæg til 'Framlegg til skrivereglar for landsmaale i skularne'* [*Suppplement to 'Recommendations for rules for Landsmaal in the schools'*], Kristiania: A. W. Brøggers Bogtrykkeri.

Hambro, Carl Joachim (1913), *Sprogets aand og bokstavens tjenere* [*The spirit of the language and the letter's servants*], Kristiania: Aschehoug.

Handagard, Idar (1901), 'Er folkemaale i byarne gode norske maalføre? Fosna-maale. Eit norskt bymaal' ['Is the popular language of the cities good Norwegian dialects? The dialect of Kristiansund. A Norwegian city dialect'], *Syn og Segn*, pp. 97–110.

Hanto, Kristian Ihlen (1986), *Ideologiar i norsk målreising* [*Ideologies in the Nynorsk movement*], Oslo: Novus.

Haraldsrud, Andreas Drolsum (2012), *Dæt læses mæd Æ. En komparativ undersøkelse av norsk og dansk danna talemål 1750–1850* [*It is read with an Æ. A comparative study of Norwegian and Danish educated speech 1750–1850*], unpublished MA thesis, University of Oslo, Department of Linguistic and Scandinavian Studies.

Haugen, Einar (1931), 'The linguistic development of Ivar Aasen's New Norse', *Publications of the Modern Language Association of America* 48, pp. 558–97.

Haugen, Einar (1965), 'Construction and reconstruction in language planning: Ivar Aasen's grammar', *Word* 21, pp. 188–207.

Haugen, Einar (1966a), *Language conflict and language planning: the case of modern Norwegian*, Cambridge, MA: Harvard University Press. (Norwegian version = *Riksspråk og folkemål: Norsk språkpolitikk i det 20. århundre*, translated by Dag Gundersen (1968), Oslo: Universitetsforlaget.)

Haugen, Einar (1966b), 'Linguistics and language planning', in W. Bright (ed.), *Sociolinguistics* (= Janua linguarum, Series maior 20), The Hague: Mouton, pp. 50–71. (Reprinted in E. Haugen [1972], *Ecology of language*, Stanford, CA: Stanford University Press, pp. 159–90.)

Haugen, Einar (1976), *The Scandinavian languages. An introduction to their history*, London: Faber and Faber Ltd. (German translation by Magnús Pétursson [1984], *Die skandinavischen Sprachen. Eine Einfürung in ihre Geschichte*, Hamburg: Helmut Buske.)

Haugen, Einar (1982), *Scandinavian language structures*, Tübingen: Max Niemeyer.

Haugen, Einar (1983), 'The implementation of corpus planning: theory and practice', in J. Cobarrubias and J. A. Fishman (eds), *Progress in language planning* (= Contribution to the sociology of language 31), Berlin: Mouton, pp. 269–89.

Haugland, Kjell (1970), 'Før Noregs Mållag' ['Before Noregs Mållag'], *Syn og Segn*, pp. 380–8.

Haugland, Kjell (1971a), 'Ei folkerørsle blir til' ['A popular movement is created'], in K. Haugland (ed.), *Målpolitiske dokument 1864–1885. Ei folkerørsle blir til [Political documents on language 1864–1885. A popular movement is created]*, Oslo: Det Norske Samlaget, pp. 7–30.

Haugland, Kjell (1971b), *Striden om sidemålsstilen. Ein studie i språk og politikk i åra 1906–07 [The struggle over the secondary essay [in high school]. A study of language and politics in the years 1906–07]*, Bergen-Oslo-Tromsø: Universitetsforlaget.

Haugland, Kjell (1974), 'Ei pressgruppe tek form: Målrørsla og

Venstrepartiet 1883–1885' ['A pressure group emerges: the Landsmaal movement and the Liberal Party 1883–1885'], *Historisk tidsskrift* 53, pp. 148–82.

Haugland, Kjell (1977a), 'Organisasjonsgjennombrotet i målarbeidet ved hundreårsskiftet' ['The organisational break-through in the work for Landsmaal around the turn of the century'], *Historisk tidsskrift* 56, pp. 19–52.

Haugland, Kjell (1977b), 'Lærarane i brodden for norsk målreising på 1800-talet. "Ta det romet som den akademiske stand fyrr hev havt"' ['The teachers in the vanguard of the struggle for Landsmaal in the 1800s. "Seize the place which was earlier occupied by the academic class"'], *Syn og Segn*, pp. 177–88.

Haugland, Kjell (1981), 'Dei eldste målorganisasjonane' ['The oldest Landsmaal organisations'], in O. Almenningen et al. (eds), *Målreising i 75 år. Noregs Mållag 1906–1981* [*Struggle for Nynorsk through 75 years. Noregs Mållag 1906–1981*], Oslo: Fonna, pp. 17–41.

Haugland, Kjell (1985), *Striden om skulemålet. Frå 1860-åra til 1902* [*The struggle over language in the schools. From the 1860s until 1902*], Oslo: Det Norske Samlaget.

Hellevik, Alf (1964), 'Norsk språknemnd blir til' ['The establishment of the Language Committee'], in A. Hellevik (ed.), *Skriftspråk i utvikling: tiårsskrift for Norsk språknemnd 1952–1962* [*Written language in development: the Language Committee 10 years, 1952–1962*] (= Skrifter 3 frå Norsk språknemnd), Oslo: Cappelen, pp. 11–38.

Hielm, Jonas Anton (1832), 'Om norsk sprog' ['On Norwegian language'], *Almindeligt norsk Maanedsskrivt* 2 (1831), pp. 461–7. (Appeared 1832.)

Hjort, Johan Bernard (1963), *Sprogstridens kvintessens* [*The quintessence of the language struggle*], Oslo: Riksmålsforbundet.

Hoel, Oddmund Løkensgard (1996), *Nasjonalisme i norsk målstrid 1848–1865* [*Nationalism in the Norwegian language struggle 1848–1865*] (= Kultur- og tradisjonsformidlande forsking, skriftserie 51), Oslo: Noregs forskingsråd.

Hoel, Oddmund Løkensgard (2011), *Mål og modernisering 1868–1940* [*Language and modernisation 1868–1940*], Oslo: Det Norske Samlaget.

Hovdan, Peder (1928), *Frå folkemål til riksmål. Blad or Noregs nyaste målsoga* [*From folk language to national language. Pages in Norway's most recent language history*], Oslo: Noregs Mållag.

Hovdan, Peder (1947), *Eit norsk Noreg* [*A Norwegian Norway*], Oslo: Det Norske Samlaget.

Hyvik, Jens Johan (2002), '"... en forbrydelse mot nationen". Tidsskriftet *Saga* (1816–20), et nasjonalt dannelsesprosjekt som mislyktes' ['"... a crime against the nation". The journal *Saga* (1816–20), a national educational project that failed'], *Historisk Tidskrift* 81, pp. 55–81.

Hyvik, Jens Johan (2009), *Språk og nasjon 1739–1868* [Language and nation 1739–1868], Oslo: Det Norske Samlaget.

Hyvik, Jens Johan (2012), '"Det klinger vel noget radikalt" – Språkprogram i tre faser' ['"It sounds a bit radical" – language programme in three stages'], in S. Bugge, J. Collett and A. Kjus (eds), *P. A. Munch: historiker og nasjonsbygger* [*P. A. Munch: historian and nation builder*], Oslo: Dreyer, pp. 152–75.

Indrebø, Gustav (1951), *Norsk målsoga* [*Norwegian language history*]. Edited by P. Hovda and P. Thorson. Bergen: John Grieg.

Indstilling (1917), *Indstilling fra Retskrivningskomiteen* [Recommendation from the Spelling Committee], Kristiania: Kirke- og Undervisningsdepartementet.

Innstilling (1966), *Innstilling om språksaken fra Komitéen til å vurdere språksituasjonen m.v. oppnevnt ved kongelig resolusjon 31. januar 1964* [*Recommendation about the language issue from the Committee for evaluating the language situation etc. appointed by royal decree, 31 January 1964*], Orkanger: Kirke- og Undervisningsdepartementet.

Jacobsen, Henrik Galberg (2010), *Ret og Skrift. Officiel dansk retskrivning 1739–2005, Bd. 1-2* [*Official Danish orthography 1739–2005, Vol. 1-2*] (= Dansk Sprognævns skrifter 42), Odense: Syddansk Universitetsforlag.

Jahr, Ernst Håkon (1976a), 'DNA og samnorskpolitikken' ['The Labour Party and the pan-Norwegian language policy'], *Kontrast: Tidsskrift for politikk, kultur, kritikk* 58, pp. 22–8. (Reprinted in E. H. Jahr [1992], *Innhogg i nyare norsk språkhistorie* [*Inroads into modern Norwegian language history*], Oslo: Novus, pp. 114–24.)

Jahr, Ernst Håkon (1976b), 'Halvdan Koht og språkstriden' ['Halvdan Koht and the language struggle'], *Mål og Makt* (published by Studentmållaget i Oslo) 6.3, pp. 6–17. (Reprinted in E. H. Jahr

[1992], *Innhogg i nyare norsk språkhistorie* [*Inroads into modern Norwegian language history*], Oslo: Novus, pp. 69–81.)

Jahr, Ernst Håkon (1978), *Østlandsmåla fram! Ei bok om rørsla Østlandsk reisning* [*Forward with the dialects of Eastern Norway! A book on the Østlandsk Reisning movement*], Tromsø-Oslo-Bergen: Universitetsforlaget.

Jahr, Ernst Håkon (1980), 'Samnorsk' ['Pan-Norwegian'], in H. F. Dahl et al. (eds), *PaxLeksikon* [*Pax Encyclopedia*] Volume 5, Oslo: Pax, pp. 350–2. (Second edition, Oslo 1982.)

Jahr, Ernst Håkon (1984), *Talemålet i skolen. En studie av drøftinger og bestemmelser om muntlig språkbruk i folkeskolen (fra 1974 til 1925)* [*Spoken language in school. A study of debates and regulations about spoken language use in primary school (from 1874 until 1925)*], Oslo: Novus.

Jahr, Ernst Håkon (1986), 'Det sosiopolitiske perspektivet på skriftspråksnormeringa i det 19. hundreåret (Noreg)' ['A sociopolitical perspective on the 19th-century planning of the written language (Norway)'], in *De nordiske skriftspråkenes utvikling på 1800-tallet, Vol. 3: Ideologier og språkstyring* [*The development of the written Nordic languages during the 1800s, Vol. 3: Ideologies and language planning*] (= Nordisk språksekretariats rapporter 7), Oslo: Nordisk språksekretariat, pp. 122–33. (Reprinted in E. H. Jahr [1992], *Innhogg i nyare norsk språkhistorie* [*Inroads into modern Norwegian language history*], Oslo: Novus, pp. 9–17.)

Jahr, Ernst Håkon (1989a), 'Language planning and language change', in L. E. Breivik and E. H. Jahr (eds), *Language change. Contributions to the study of its causes* (= Trends in linguistics, Studies and monographs 43), Berlin/New York: Mouton de Gruyter, pp. 99–113. (Reprinted in P. Trudgill and J. Chesire (eds) [1998], *The sociolinguistics reader, Volume 1: Multilinguialism and variation*, London: Arnold, pp. 263-75.)

Jahr, Ernst Håkon (1989b), 'Limits of language planning? Norwegian language planning revisited', *International Journal of the Sociology of Language* 80, pp. 33–9.

Jahr, Ernst Håkon (1992), 'Samnorskideologi og samnorskpolitikk i nyare norsk målsoge – fram til skipinga av Landslaget for språklig samling' ['Pan-Norwegian ideology and pan-Norwegian policy in recent Norwegian language history – until the establishment of the organization the National League for Language Unification'], in

E. H. Jahr (1992), *Innhogg i nyare norsk språkhistorie [Inroads into modern Norwegian language history]*, Oslo: Novus, pp. 144–8.

Jahr, Ernst Håkon (1994), *Utsyn over norsk språkhistorie etter 1814 [Overview of Norwegian language history from 1814]*, 2nd revised edition, Oslo: Novus. (First edition 1989.)

Jahr, Ernst Håkon (1996), 'Språkstrid og språkplanlegging i Norge på 1970- og 1980-tallet – bakgrunn og innhold' ['Language struggle and language planning in Norway in the 1970s and 1980s – background and contents'], in L. Elmevik, B.-L. Gunnarsson, B. Melander and M. Thelander (eds), *Samspel & variation. Språkliga studier tillägnade Bengt Nordberg på 60-årsdagen [Interaction & variation. Linguistic studies for Bengt Nordberg on his 60th birthday]*, Uppsala: Institutionen för nordiska språk, Uppsala universitet, pp. 167–83.

Jahr, Ernst Håkon (1997a), 'The fate of Samnorsk: A social dialect experiment in language planning', in M. Clyne (ed.), *Undoing and redoing corpus planning* (= Contributions to the sociology of language 78), Berlin/New York: Mouton de Gruyter, pp. 215–48.

Jahr, Ernst Håkon (1997b), 'On the use of dialects in Norway', in H. Ramisch and K. Wynne (eds), *Language in time and space. A festschrift for Wolfgang Viereck on his sixtieth birthday, 4 September 1997* (= Zeitschrift für Dialektologie und Linguistik – Beihefte), Stuttgart: Franz Steiner, pp. 363–9.

Jahr, Ernst Håkon (2001), 'Historical sociolinguistics: the role of Low German language contact in the Scandinavian typological shift of the Late Middle Ages', *Lingua Posnaniensis* 43, pp. 95–104.

Jahr, Ernst Håkon (2005), 'Artikkelen "Tove Bull" i Norsk Biografisk Leksikon i ein språkstridskontekst – som døme på "fri sprogutvikling" og "mindre brukte former i bokmål"' ['The article "Tove Bull" in the Norwegian Biographical Encyclopedia in the context of the language struggle – as an example of "free development of language" and "lesser-used word forms in Bokmål"'], in G. Alhaug, E. Mørck and A.-K. Pedersen (eds), *Mot rikare mål å trå. Festskrift til Tove Bull [To strive for a richer goal. Festschrift for Tove Bull]*, Oslo: Novus, pp. 1–4.

Jahr, Ernst Håkon (2008), 'On the reasons for dialect maintenance in Norway', *Sociolinguistica* 22, pp. 157–70.

Jahr, Ernst Håkon (2010), 'Kløyvd infinitiv i dei norske skriftnormalane' ['The dual/cleft infinitive in the Norwegian written standards'], in K. Jóhannesson et al. (eds), *Bo65. Festskrift till Bo Ralph* [*Bo65. Festschrift for Bo Ralph*] (= Meijerbergs arkiv för svensk ordforskning 39), Göteborg: Göteborgs universitet, Meijerbergs institut, pp. 124–36.

Jahr, Ernst Håkon (2012), 'To språkkontaktendringer i bergensdialekta – eller ikke? Om den tonelagsløse ringen rundt Bergen og om preteritum på –*et*' ['Two language contact induced changes in the Bergen dialect – or not? On the non-word-tone area around Bergen, and about preterites in –*et*'], in H. van der Liet and M. Norde (eds), *Language for its own sake. Essays on language and literature offered to Harry Perridon* (= Amsterdam contributions to Scandinavian studies 8), Amsterdam: Universiteit van Amsterdam, Scandinavisch Instituut, pp. 359–74.

Jahr, Ernst Håkon and Karol Janicki (1995), The function of a standard variety – a comparative study of Norwegian and Polish, *International Journal of the Sociology of Language* 115, pp. 25–45.

Jahr, Ernst Håkon and Ingrid Schanche (1988), 'Jamstillingsvedtaket i 1885 – forstår vi det nå?' ['The Language Equality Resolution of 1885 – do we understand it now?'], *Norsk Lingvistisk Tidsskrift* 6, pp. 139–50. (Reprinted in E. H. Jahr [1992], *Innhogg i nyare norsk språkhistorie* [*Inroads into modern Norwegian language history*], Oslo: Novus, pp. 18–27.)

Johnsen, Egil Børre (2003), *Fola fola Blakken: En biografi om Nordahl Rolfsen* [*A biography of Nordahl Rolfsen*], Oslo: Andresen & Butenschøn.

Johnsen, Egil Børre (2006), *Unorsk og norsk. Knud Knudsen. En beretning om bokmålets far* [*Non-Norwegian and Norwegian. Knud Knudsen. An account of the father of Bokmål*], Tvedestrand: Bokbyen Forlag.

Kaplan, Robert B. and Richard B. Baldauf Jr (1997), *Language planning from practice to theory* (= Multilingual Matters 108), Clevedon, England: Multilingual Matters Ltd.

Kaplan, Robert B. and Richard B. Baldauf Jr (eds) (2005), *Language planning and policy in Europe, Vol. 1: Hungary, Finland and Sweden*, Clevedon-Buffalo-Toronto: Multilingual Matters Ltd.

Kaplan, Robert B. and Richard B. Baldauf Jr (eds) (2008), *Language planning and policy in Europe, Vol. 3: The Baltic states, Ireland and Italy*, Clevedon-Buffalo-Toronto: Multilingual Matters Ltd.

Kirke- og Undervisningsdepartementet (1938), *Ny rettskrivning 1938*.

Bokmål. Regler og ordliste [*New orthographic standard 1938. Bokmål. Rules and word list*], Oslo: Olaf Norlis Forlag.

Kjeldstadli, Knut (1994), *Et splittet samfunn: 1905–35* [A divided society: 1905–35] (= Aschehougs norgeshistorie vol. 10), Oslo: Aschehoug.

Klassekampen, 26 August 2013. Oslo.

Kloss, Heinz (1967), 'Abstand-languages and Ausbau-languages', *Anthropological linguistics* 9, pp. 29–41.

Kloss, Heinz (1969), *Research possibilities on group bilingualism: A report*. Quebec: International center for research on bilingualism.

Knudsen, Knud (1845), 'Om Lydene, Lydtegnene og Retskrivningen i det norske Sprog' ['On sounds, phonetic symbols and orthography in Norwegian'], *NOR – Tidsskrift for Videnskab og Literatur* 3.2 (1844), pp. 39–122. Christiania. (Appeared 1845.)

Knudsen, Knud (1850), 'Om Norskhed i vor Tale og Skrift' ['On Norwegianness in our speech and writing'], *Norsk Tidsskrift for Videnskab og Litteratur* 4, pp. 205–73.

Knudsen, Knud (1856), *Haandbog i dansk-norsk Sproglære* [*Handbook of Dano-Norwegian grammar*], Kristiania: Abelsted.

Knudsen, Knud [1861], *Om norsk Uttale og Oplæsning* [*On Norwegian pronunciation and reading aloud*]. [Christiania.] (First published in *Den Norske Folkeskole*, 1861.)

Knudsen, Knud (1862), *Er Norsk det samme som Dansk?* [*Is Norwegian the Same as Danish?*] (= Indbydelsesskrift til den offentlige examen ved Kristiania Kathedralskole), Kristiania: Steenske Bogtrykkeri.

Knudsen, Knud (1867), *Det norske målstræv* [*The Norwegian language endeavour*], Kristiania: Trykt på forfatterens kostning hos Brøgger & Christie.

Knudsen, Knud (1876), *Den landsgyldige norske Udtale* [*Nationwide Norwegian pronunciation*], Kristiania: Trykt på forfatterens kostning hos A. W. Brøgger.

Knudsen, Knud (1887), *Kortfattet redegjørelse for det dansknorske målstræv* [*A brief account of the Dano-Norwegian language endeavour*]. Kristiania: Chr. H. Knudsen.

Knudsen, Trygve (1923), *P.A. Munch og samtidens norske sprogstrev* [*P.A. Munch and the contemporary Norwegian language endeavour*], Kristiania: Gyldendal.

Knudsen, Trygve (1967), 'Phrases of style and language in the works of Henrik Ibsen', in T. Knudsen (ed.), *Skrifttradisjon og litteraturmål. Artikler og avhandlinger i utvalg. Festskrift i anledning av professor dr. Trygve Knudsens 70 års dag 23. juni 1967*, Oslo: Universitetsforlaget, pp. 143–72. (First published in *Scandinavica* 2, 1963.)

Koht, Halvdan (1921), *Arbeidarreising og målspørsmål* [*Working class uprising and language issues*], Kristiania: Det norske Arbeiderpartis Forlag.

Kulbrandstad, Lars Anders (2011), 'National or general tolerance for variation. Attitudes to dialect and foreign accent in the media', in R. M. Millar and M. Durham (eds), *Applied linguistics, global and local*, London: Scitsiugnil Press, pp. 173–82.

Kvamen, Ingolf (1958), *Målpolitikken i dag* [*The Nynorsk policy today*], Oslo: Ivar Aasen-ringen i Oslo.

Langslet, Lars Roar (1999), *I kamp for norsk kultur. Riksmålsbevegelsens historie gjennom 100 år* [*Battling for Norwegian culture. The history of the Riksmål movement over 100 years*], Oslo: Riksmålsforbundet.

Larsen, Amund B. (1907), *Kristiania bymål. Vulgærsproget med henblik på den utvungne dagligtale* [*The urban dialect of Oslo. The working-class dialect compared with casual daily speech*], Kristiania: Cammermeyer.

Larson, Karen A. (1985), *Learning without lessons: Socialization and language change in Norway*, Lanham: University Press of America.

Lind, Asbjørn (1975), *Partiet Høyre og norsk språkstrid* [*The Conservative Party (Høyre) and the Norwegian language controversy*], unpublished Cand. Philol. thesis, University of Oslo, Department of Scandinavian Studies.

Linn, Andrew Robert (1997), *Constructing the grammars of a language: Ivar Aasen and nineteenth-century Norwegian linguistics* (= The Henry Sweet Society Studies in the history of linguistics 4), Münster: Nodus.

Listov, Andreas (1866), *Ordsamling fra den norske æsthetiske Literatur siden Aaret 1842* [*Norwegian literary vocabulary from after the year 1842*]. Kjøbenhavn: Gyldendalske Boghandel.

Lockertsen, Roger (2007), *Namnet på byen Trondheim: ein språkhistorisk og faghistorisk analyse* [*The name of the city of Trondheim: A historical linguistic analysis*], Oslo: Novus.

Lomheim, Sylfest (2007), *Språkreisa. Norsk gjennom to tusen år* [*A linguistic journey. Norwegian over two thousand years*], Oslo: Damm.

Mesthrie, Rajend, Joan Swann, Ana Deumert and William L.

Leap (2009), *Introducing sociolinguistics*, 2nd edition, Edinburgh: Edinburgh University Press.

Meyen, Fritz (1932), *'Riksmålsforbundet' und sein Kampf gegen das Landsmål: ein Abschnitt aus Norwegens innerer Geschichte* ['*Riksmålforbundet' and its struggle against Landsmål: A part of Norwegian domestic history*], Oslo: I kommusjon hos Riksmaalsforbundet.

Moe, Moltke (1909), 'Nationalitet og kultur' ['Nationality and culture'], *Samtiden* 20, pp. 17–28.

Munch, Peter Andreas (1832), 'Norsk Sprogreformation' ['Norwegian language reform'], *Vidar* 1, pp. 5–8; and 2, pp. 12–15.

Munch, Peter Andreas (1848), 'Den norske Folkesprogs Grammatik af Ivar Aasen' ['Review of: Grammar of the Norwegian people's language, by Ivar Aasen'], *Norsk Tidsskrift for Videnskab og Litteratur* 2, pp. 282–98.

Nielsen, May-Brith Ohman (2011), *Norvegr. Norges historie – bind IV, etter 1914* [*Norvegr. A history of Norway – volume IV, after 1914*], Oslo: Aschehoug.

Norsk Skoleblad (1973), No. 25. Oslo.

Nygaard, Rolf R. (1945), *Fra dansk-norsk til norsk riksmål. Rettskrivningsstrevet i bokmålet inntil 1907* [*From Dano-Norwegian to Norwegian Riksmål. Reform initiatives for bokmål up to 1907*], Oslo: J. G. Tanum.

Opsahl, Toril (2010), *'Egentlig alle kan bidra!' – en samling sosiolingvistiske studier av strukturelle trekk ved norsk i multietniske ungdomsmiljøer i Oslo* ['*Really, everybody can contribute!' – a collection of sociolinguistic studies of structural features of Norwegian amongst multiethnic youth groups in Oslo*], unpublished Ph.D. dissertation, University of Oslo, Faculty of Humanities.

Østby, Andreas Eilert (2005), *Kebabnorsk ordbok* [*Kebab Norwegian dictionary*], Oslo: Gyldendal.

Øverland, Arnulf (1940), *Er vårt sprog avskaffet?* [*Has our language been abolished?*], Oslo: Aschehoug.

Øverland, Arnulf (1948), *Hvor ofte skal vi skifte sprog?* [*How often shall we change language?*], Oslo: Aschehoug.

Øverland, Arnulf (1949), *Bokmålet – et avstumpet landsmål* [*Bokmål – a crippled Landsmål*], Oslo: Aschehoug.

Paul, Hermann (1880), *Prinzipien der Sprachgeschichte* [*Principles in language history*]. Halle: Max Niemeyer. (Second edition, 1886.)

Petersen, Erling (1977), *Om 1917-rettskrivningen. Språkholdninger og språksyn i den offentlige debatten* [*On the 1917 language reform. Language attitudes and language views in the public debate*], unpublished Cand. Philol. thesis, University of Bergen, Department of Scandinavian Studies.

Pettersen, Egil (1993), *Språknormering og forfatterne. Ortografi og morfembruk hos ti bokmålsforfattere for hvert av årene 1937, 1957 og 1977* [*Language planning and the authors. The orthography and morphology of ten Bokmål authors for each of the years 1937, 1957 and 1977*] (= *Eigenproduksjon* No. 49. University of Bergen, Department of Scandinavian Studies), Utgitt av Norsk språkråd.

Popp, Daniel (1977), *Asbjørnsen's linguistic reform. A study of the individual writer's role in written developments. I. Orthography*. Oslo-Bergen-Tromsø: Universitetsforlaget.

Pryser, Tore (1993), 'The Thranite movement in Norway 1849–1851', *Scandinavian Journal of History* 18, pp. 169–82.

Rambø, Gro-Renée (1999): *Bokmålsreformen i 1981 – med særlig vekt på Særutvalgets arbeid* [*The Bokmål reform of 1981 – with special emphasis on the work of the Special Committee*] (= Forskningsserien nr. 20), Kristiansand: Høgskolen i Agder.

Riad, Tomas (2006), 'Scandinavian accent typology', *Sprachtypol. Univ. Forsch. (STUF)*, Berlin 59.1, pp. 36–55.

Riksmaalsforbundet (1913), *Utredning av nogen sprogspørsmaal* [*Report on some language issues*], Kristiania: Olaf Bryde.

Riksmålsvernet (1958), *Kritikk av 'Framlegg til læreboknormal 1957. Fra Norsk språknemnd'* [*Review of 'Recommendation for a New Textbook Standard' 1957. From the Language Committee*]. Oslo.

Rogne, Magne (1998), *Målstrid og politikk i 1920-åra. Dei politiske partia og målstriden på Stortinget i perioden 1919–1930* [*Language struggle and politics in the 1920s. The political parties and the language struggle in Parliament in the period 1919–1930*], unpublished Cand. Philol. thesis, University of Oslo, Department of Scandinavian Studies and Comparative Literature.

Rolfsen, Nordahl (ed.) (1892), *Læsebog for folkeskolen. Første Del* [*Reader for the primary school. First part*], Kristiania: Jacob Dybwad.

Rykkja, Åshild (1978), *Det Norske Arbeiderparti og språkstriden, 1903–1937* [*The Norwegian Labour Party and the language struggle, 1903–1937*], unpublished Cand. Philol. thesis, University of Oslo, Department of Scandinavian Studies. Oslo.

Seip, Didrik Arup (1913), 'Storm Munchs *Saga* og den første maal-strid i Norge' ['Storm Munch's *Saga* and the first language struggle in Norway'], in *Festskrift til Alf Torp* [*Festschrift for Alf Torp*], Kristiania: Aschehoug, pp. 122–36.

Seip, Didrik Arup (1914), *Norskhet i sproget hos Wergeland og hans samtid* [*Norwegian traits in the language of Wergeland and his contemporaries*], Kristiania: Aschehoug.

Seip, Didrik Arup (1916a), 'Stilen i Bjørnsons bondefortellinger' ['Style in Bjørnson's peasant stories'], *Edda* 5, pp. 1–21.

Seip, Didrik Arup (1916b), *Grundlaget for det norske riksmaal* [*The basis of Norwegian Riksmål*] (= Tiltrædelsesforelæsning 28 April 1916 paa Universitetet), Kristiania: Norli.

Seip, Didrik Arup (1917), *Ett mål i Norge. Målstriden avgjort av denne generation?* [*One language in Norway. The language struggle decided by this generation?*], Kristiania: Norli.

Seip, Didrik Arup (1930), *Trondhjems bynavn* [*Trondheim's city name*], Trondhjem: F. Brun.

Seip, Didrik Arup (1971), *Norwegische sprachgeschichte* [*Norwegian language history*] (= Grundriss der Germanischen Philologie 19). Berlin: Walter de Gruyter. (First Norwegian edition 1931; 2nd edition 1955.)

Skard, Sigmund (1963), *Målstrid og massekultur* [*Language struggle and mass culture*], Oslo: Det Norske Samlaget.

Skard, Vemund (1949), *Frå Dølen til Fedraheimen. Målstriden 1870–1877* [*From 'Dølen' to 'Fedraheimen'. The language struggle 1870–1877*], Oslo: Det Norske Samlaget.

Skirbekk, Sigurd (1967), 'Ideologier i språkstriden' ['Ideologies in the language struggle'], *Kontrast* 8, pp. 106–17.

Skirbekk, Sigurd, Bjarne Fidjestøl and Otto Hageberg (eds) (1967), *Kontur og kontrast. Ti essays om språk og kultur* [*Contour and contrast. Ten essays on language and culture*], Oslo: Det Norske Samlaget.

Søilen, Oddmund (1978), *Halvdan Koht: Språk og historie. En undersøkelse av Halvdan Kohts målpolitikk og målreisingsarbeid* [*Halvdan Koht: Language and history. A study of Halvdan Koht's language policy and work for the promotion of Nynorsk*], unpublished Cand. Philol. thesis, University of Bergen, Department of Scandinavian Studies.

Steinset, Åge and Jo Kleiven (1975), *Språk og identitet* [*Language and identity*], Oslo: Det Norske Samlaget.

Stortingstidende (1937), *Stortingstidende inneholdende seksogåttiende ordentlige stortings forhandlinger 1937. Forhandlinger i Stortinget vol. 7B* [*Parliamentary proceedings 1937*], Oslo: Centraltrykkeriet.

Strand, Vibeke Sonja (1979), *Landslaget for språklig samling* [*The League for Language Unification*], unpublished Cand. Philol. thesis, University of Oslo, Department of Scandinavian Studies.

Svendsen, Åsmund (2013), *Halvdan Koht. Veien mot framtiden. En biografi* [*Halvdan Koht. The road to the future. A biography*], Oslo: Cappelen Damm.

Taule, Ragnvald H. (1973), *Arnulf Øverland om språk og språksituasjon. Sentrale sider ved riksmålsagitasjonen i etterkrigstida* [*Arnulf Øverland on language and the language situation. Central aspects of the post-war agitation for Riksmål*], unpublished Cand. Philol. thesis, University of Bergen, Department of Scandinavian Studies.

Tilråding (1935), *Tilråding om ny rettskrivning. Fra den departementale rettskrivningsnevnd av 1934* [*Recommendation for a new orthography. From the Ministry's language committee of 1934*], Trondheim: Kirke- og Undervisningsdepartementet. (Cf. also [1936], *Tilleggstilråding om ny rettskrivning. Fra den departementale rettskrivningsnevnd av 1934* [*Supplementary recommendation for a new orthography. From the Ministry's language committee of 1934*], Stavanger: Kirke- og Undervisningsdepartementet.)

Tjelle, Arne (1994), 'Rettskrivinga av 1941. Bakgrunn, politisk spel og ideologisk analyse' ['The orthography of 1941. Background, political games and ideological analysis'], *Nordica Bergensia* 2, University of Bergen.

Torp, Arne and Lars S. Vikør (1993), *Hovuddrag i norsk språkhistorie* [*Main features of Norwegian language history*], Oslo: Ad Notam Gyldendal.

Trudgill, Peter (1986), *Dialects in contact* [= Language in society 10], Oxford: Blackwell.

Trudgill, Peter (2002), *Sociolinguistic variation and change*. Edinburgh: Edinburgh University Press.

Tryti, Ivar (1953), *Rettskrivningsstrevet i norsk riksmål 1907–1917* [*Orthographic reform in Norwegian Riksmål 1907–1917*], unpublished Cand. Philol. thesis, University of Oslo, Department of Scandinavian Studies.

Tvinnereim, Jon (1973), 'Då landsmålet vart kristna' ['When Landsmål was christened'], *Syn og Segn*, pp. 604–7.

Vaagland, Per Ivar (1982), *Målrørsla og reformarbeidet i trettiåra* [*The Nynorsk movement and work towards reform in the 1930s*], Oslo: Det Norske Samlaget.

Vannebo, Kjell Ivar (1979), 'Omgrepet *Samnorsk*' ['The concept of *Samnorsk*'], in L. S. Vikør and G. Wiggen (eds), *Språklig samling på folkemåls grunn* [*Language unification on the basis of the people's language*], Oslo: Novus, pp. 220–34.

Vannebo, Kjell Ivar (1984), *En nasjon av skriveføre. Om utviklinga fram mot allmenn skriveferdighet på 1800-tallet* [*A nation of literates. On the development towards general literacy during the 1800s*] (= Oslo-studier i språkvitenskap 2), Oslo: Novus.

Venås, Kjell (1984), *For Noreg og Ivar Aasen: Gustav Indrebø i arbeid og strid* [*For Norway and Ivar Aasen: Gustav Indrebø at work and conflict*], Oslo: Novus.

Venås, Kjell (1992a), *I Aasens fotefar: Marius Hægstad* [*In the footsteps of Aasen: Marius Hægstad*], Oslo: Novus.

Venås, Kjell (1992b), 'Dialect and standards in Norway', in J. A.van Leuvensteijn and J. B. Berns (eds), *Dialect and standard language in the English, Dutch, German and Norwegian language areas* (= Proceedings of the colloquium Dialect and Standard Language, Amsterdam, 15–18 October 1990/Koninklijke Nederlandse Akademie van Wetenschappen Verhandelingen, Afd. Letterkunde, Nieuwe Reeks, deel 150), Amsterdam: Royal Netherlands Academy of Arts and Sciences, pp. 337–50.

Venås, Kjell (1996), *Då tida var fullkomen: Ivar Aasen* [*When the time was ripe: Ivar Aasen*], Oslo: Novus.

Venås, Kjell (1997), 'Ivar Aasen (1896–1996): Eit minneforedrag' ['Ivar Aasen (1896–1996): a memorial lecture'], *Årbok 1996. Det Kongelige Norske Videnskabers Selskabs Forhandlinger 1996* [*Yearbook 1996. The Royal Norwegian Society of Sciences and Letters*]. Trondheim: Det Kongelige Norske Videnskabers Selskab, pp. 149–60.

Vikør, Lars S. (1975), *The New Norse language movement*, Oslo: Novus.

Vikør, Lars S. and Geirr Wiggen (eds) (1979), *Språklig samling på folkemåls grunn* [*Language unification on the basis of the people's language*], Oslo: Novus.

Vinje, Finn-Erik (1978), *Et språk i utvikling. Noen hovedlinjer i norsk språkhistorie fra reformasjonen til våre dager* [*A developing language. Some main directions in Norwegian language history from the Reformation until our time*], Oslo: Aschehough.

Walton, Stephen J. (1987), *Farewell the Spirit Craven: Ivar Aasen and national romanticism*, Oslo: Det Norske Samlaget.

Walton, Stephen J. (1996), *Ivar Aasens kropp* [*Ivar Aasen's body*], Oslo: Det Norske Samlaget.

Waschnitius, Victor (1921), 'A. O. Vinjes Sprachentwicklung' ['A. O. Vinje's language development'], *Edda* 14, pp. 161–201.

Wergeland, Henrik [1832] (1835), 'Om norsk Sprogreformation' ['On Norwegian language reform'], *Bondevennen* 1, pp. 132–67.

Wetås, Åse (2000), *Namneskiftet Kristiania – Oslo* [*The name change Kristiania – Oslo*], Oslo: Novus.

Wiggen, Geirr (ed.) (1973), *Ny målstrid. Artikler og innlegg om språk, samfunn og ideologi* [*New language struggle. Articles on language, society and ideology*], Oslo: Novus. (Second expanded edition, 1974.)

List of terms of language varieties

AASEN STANDARD (*Aasennormalen*)
The name of the final version of the Landsmaal standard which emerged from Aasen's 1864 *Norwegian Grammar* and 1873 *Norwegian Dictionary*. This standard was never officially recognised by the authorities. The first officially authorised Landsmaal standard was the 1901 Hægstad Standard.

BOKMÅL (*Bokmål*)
Used from 1929 for the written standard which until then was called Riksmål.

COMMON LANGUAGE (*Fællessproget*)
Used instead of 'Danish' to refer to the usual written standard in the first half of the nineteenth century. Even 'mother tongue' (*modersmaalet*) was used to refer to Danish in the same period.

DANISH (*Dansk*)
The written standard used in Norway (before and) after 1814 until 1862. From 1862, it was called Dano-Norwegian.

DANO-NORWEGIAN (*Dansk-norsk*)
Used for the written standard from 1862 until 1907. From 1862, Danish as used in Norway was unilaterally altered by Norwegian authorities according to Norwegian plans and wishes, resulting in 1907 in Norwegian Riksmaal.

DANO-NORWEGIAN CREOLOID

Used in this book to designate the spoken variety which developed mainly in the eighteenth century as a result of language contact and accommodation between (spoken) Norwegian and (written) Danish. It was grammatically simplified compared to both Norwegian rural dialects and written Danish. Its prosody and phonology were clearly non-Danish; however, its morphology and word forms were taken mainly from written Danish. It was developed and used by the upper-middle classes throughout the country: government officials, civil servants and a few very rich merchants. During the nineteenth and twentieth centuries it was known by several different names and terms: *den dannede dagligtale* 'the educated casual speech', *talt riksmål* 'spoken Riksmål', *dannet tale* 'educated speech', and others. Between 1917 and 1938, the most frequently used written Riksmål standard reflected this spoken variety almost completely. During that time, many people who wanted to change their dialect acquired this variety as their spoken idiom, regardless of whether they belonged to the upper-middle classes or not. In this book, we use the term 'upper-middle-class speech' for 'spoken Riksmål' throughout. This is obviously a rather gross generalisation. It should always be kept in mind that quite a number of people other than members of the upper-middle classes – at least up until the 1970s – opted to use spoken Riksmål if, for some reason, they wanted to speak something other than their local dialect. After the 1970s, however, this spoken variety seems to have lost most of its earlier more or less unmarked status as 'standard Norwegian' to written official Bokmål.

HÆGSTAD STANDARD (*Hægstadnormalen*)

The first Landsmaal standard, officially authorised for use in schools in 1901. Named after Professor Marius Hægstad, who recommended alterations to the Aasen Standard that were accepted by the Ministry of Church and Education. The Hægstad Standard brought Landsmaal closer to contemporary dialects and was the official standard until the language reform of 1917.

LANDSMAAL/LANDSMÅL

The name given by Aasen to his proposed written standard in 1853. According to Aasen, this term was to be interpreted as 'the language of the country/realm' (*i landet* = 'of the country'), but another possible interpretation was 'the language in the countryside' (*på landet*).

In the second decade of the twentieth century, one therefore saw a growing discontent with the term among Landsmaal supporters. This constituted part of the background for the change of name to *Nynorsk* (and *Bokmål*) in 1929.

MIDLAND STANDARD (*Midlandsnormalen*)
Special Landsmaal standard developed by Arne Garborg and Rasmus Flo towards the end of the nineteenth century. This standard represented a considerable departure from the Aasen Standard as it was based heavily on the central ('mid') mountain dialects. Garborg and Flo recommended this as a replacement for the Aasen Standard, but the Ministry of Church and Education decided instead on the alternative put forth by Professor Marius Hægstad (see HÆGSTAD STANDARD). When the Ministry authorised the Hægstad Standard in 1901 for use in schools, it also agreed that the Midland Standard could be used by pupils in their (examination) essays. However, it could not be used in school textbooks.

MODERATE BOKMÅL (*Moderat bokmål*)
One variety of official Bokmål from 1938 onwards, which included few (or as few as possible) specific morphological features and word forms from southeastern and working-class dialects, and few forms parallel to those in Nynorsk. This variety was sometimes called Conservative Bokmål (*Konservativt bokmål*), since it was closer to upper-middle-class speech than Radical Bokmål (see below). The sociolinguistic difference between Moderate and Radical Bokmål was significant.

NYNORSK (*Nynorsk*)
Used from 1929 for the written standard which until then was called *Landsmål*.

OBLIGATORY LANDSMÅL (*Obligatorisk landsmål*)
Landsmål with obligatory forms (*landsmål med obligatoriske former*), the 1917 variety of Landsmål with the fewest changes in relation to the 1901 Hægstad Standard.

OBLIGATORY RIKSMÅL (*Obligatorisk riksmål*)
Riksmål with obligatory forms (*Riksmål med obligatoriske former*), the 1917 variety of the written Riksmål standard closest to and almost

completely reflecting upper-middle-class speech. This variety is the stage of the Riksmål/Bokmål standard which was later considered by the Riksmål movement to represent the ideal form of the Bokmål standard.

OPTIONAL LANDSMÅL (*Valfritt landsmål*)
Landsmål with optional forms (*Landsmål med valfrie former*), the 1917 variety of Landsmål with as many southeastern rural and urban dialect forms and morphological features as possible, and thus approaching the Optional Riksmål standard.

OPTIONAL RIKSMÅL (*Valgfritt riksmål*)
Riksmål with optional forms (*Riksmål med valgfrie former*), the 1917 variety of the written Riksmål standard which included as many southeastern and working-class dialect forms as possible, as well as forms parallel to those in Landsmål (*cf.* also Radical Bokmål). This variety of Riksmål was thus sociolinguistically closer to Landsmål and quite removed from upper-middle-class speech. In 1918 and 1919, many primary schools with Riksmål as their main standard, especially in the southeastern and northern parts of the country, introduced the Optional Riksmål variety. This caused the Riksmål movement to focus their opposition in the 1920s on the Optional Riksmål variety more than against Landsmål.

PAN-NORWEGIAN *see* SAMNORSK

RADICAL BOKMÅL (*Radikalt bokmål*)
One variety of official Bokmål from 1938 onwards, which included many (or as many as possible) specific morphological features and word forms from southeastern and working-class dialects, as well as forms parallel to those in Nynorsk. This Bokmål variety represented the sociolinguistic direction stipulated by the Labour Party programme of the 1930s. Because of the salient sociolinguistic features of Radical Bokmål, it was constantly referred to as *Samnorsk* (pan-Norwegian) by the Riksmål movement during the post-war period.

RIKSMAAL/RIKSMÅL (*Riksmaal/Riksmål*)
Name of the Dano-Norwegian written standard from 1907, used for the first time around the turn of the century. Many Riksmål

supporters were not happy with the 1929 change of name to Bokmål for their standard. In the post-war period, and up to the present, 'Riksmål' has been used as a term for the private standard promoted by the organisation *Riksmålsforbundet* and Riksmål supporters, in competition with the official Bokmål standard.

SAMNORSK (*Samnorsk*)
This term refers to Parliament's single-standard goal from 1915 onwards, which was abandoned in 2002. Before World War II, the term referred to the prospective outcome of the pan-Norwegian policy; after the war, it became more or less synonymous with Radical Bokmål.

SPOKEN RIKSMÅL (*talt riksmål*) *see* DANO-NORWEGIAN CREOLOID

UPPER-MIDDLE-CLASS SPEECH *see* DANO-NORWEGIAN CREOLOID

Timeline for the different written varieties of Norwegian

	Bokmål's development	Nynorsk's development
1814	Danish/the 'mother tongue'	
1853		Landsmaal
1862	Dano-Norwegian	Landsmaal
1864/1873	Dano-Norwegian	Landsmaal Aasen Standard
1901	Dano-Norwegian	Landsmaal Hægstad Standard (Midland Standard)
1907	Riksmaal	Landsmaal
1917	Riksmål, Obligatory Riksmål, Optional Riksmål	Landsmål, Obligatory Landsmål, Optional Landsmål
1929	Bokmål	Nynorsk
1938	Moderate Bokmål, Radical Bokmål	Nynorsk
1950s	Moderate Bokmål, Riksmål, Radical Bokmål, 'Samnorsk'	Nynorsk
1981/2005/ 2012	Moderate Bokmål/Riksmål, Radical Bokmål	Nynorsk

Timeline of important events for language planning and conflict in modern Norway

1814	End of the Dano-Norwegian union, bilateral union with Sweden. Norwegian Constitution the most democratic in Europe at the time, birth of the modern Norwegian nation.
1816	The journal *Saga* founded.
1832	Henrik Wergeland's 'On Norwegian language reform' ('Om Norsk Sprogreformation', published 1835); P. A. Munch's 'Norwegian language reform' ('Norsk sprogreformation').
1836	Ivar Aasen's 'On our written language' ('Om vort skriftsprog').
1841	First volume of folk tales collected by Asbjørnsen and Moe.
1842–6	Ivar Aasen's fieldwork in large parts of the country.
1845	Knud Knudsen's 'On sounds, phonetic symbols, and orthography in Norwegian' ('Om lydene, lydtegnene og retskrivningen i det Norske sprog').
1848	Ivar Aasen's *Grammar of the Norwegian People's Language* (*Det norske Folkesprogs Grammatik*).
1850	Ivar Aasen's *Dictionary of the Norwegian People's Language* (*Ordbog over det norske Folkesprog*); Knud Knudsen's 'On Norwegianness in our speech and writing' ('Om Norskhed i vor tale og skrift').
1853	Ivar Aasen's *Samples of the Landsmaal in Norway* (*Prøver af Landsmaalet i Norge*), first suggestion of a Landsmaal standard.
1856	Knud Knudsen's *Handbook of Dano-Norwegian Grammar* (*Haandbog i dansk-norsk Sproglære*).

1858	Aasmund O. Vinje launched the Landsmaal magazine *Dølen* ('The Dalesman').
1862	The first official language reform: orthographic changes to Danish as it was used in Norway, resulting in Dano-Norwegian.
1864	Ivar Aasen's *Norwegian Grammar* (*Norsk Grammatik*).
1868	The first Landsmaal organisations are established.
1870	Aasmund O. Vinje dies and *Dølen* ceases publication.
1873	Ivar Aasen's *Norwegian Dictionary* (*Norsk Ordbog*). Together with the 1864 grammar, this establishes the 'Aasen Standard'.
1878	Parliament passes a resolution that the oral language used in schools should be the 'tongue of the children', that is the local dialect; this principle was included in the School Acts of 1915 (rural schools) and 1917 (town and city schools).
1884	Parliamentary rule introduced, the government is now dependent on Parliament's support.
1885	Parliament passes the 'Language Equality Resolution' which establishes the formal equality of Dano-Norwegian and Landsmaal.
1887	The Ministry of Church and Education decrees that upper-middle-class speech (the Dano-Norwegian creoloid) is the norm for reading Dano-Norwegian texts aloud in schools.
1892	The Amendment of the School Act, giving local school boards throughout the country the authority to decide which of the two official written standards to use in their schools. Nordahl Rolfsen's Dano-Norwegian reader for primary schools appears in its first edition, with many unauthorised word forms from upper-middle-class speech.
1893	The Ministry of Church and Education gives pupils permission to use the unauthorised word forms found in Rolfsen's reader in their written essays. By doing so, the principle of parallel forms in the standard(s) is introduced.
1901	The first officially authorised Landsmaal standard: the 'Hægstad Standard'.
1905	The union with Sweden is dissolved.
1906	The nationwide organisation for Landsmaal is established: *Norigs Maallag* (now: *Noregs Mållag*).
1907	Reform of Dano-Norwegian with upper-middle-class

speech as the basis for the changes, resulting in Norwegian Riksmaal. Parliament introduces the requirement for an essay written in Landsmaal as part of the high-school examination. Establishment of the nationwide organisation for Riksmaal supporters: *Riksmaalsforbundet* (now: *Riksmålsforbundet*).

1909   Recommendation from the Eitrem Committee, appointed to investigate changes to bring Riksmaal and Landsmaal closer to each other. Moltke Moe's 'Nationality and culture' ('Nationalitet og kultur'), arguing for a pan-Norwegian solution.

1910   Minor reform of Landsmaal.

1911–12 The 'Grimstad Affair' about the language of oral instruction in schools.

1913   The Torp Committee appointed by the Ministry of Church and Education to prepare a reform of both Riksmaal and Landsmaal.

1915   Parliament passes an amendment to the School Act securing the principle from 1878, giving pupils in rural schools the right to use their own dialects. The same right for children in town and city schools follows in 1917.

1916   The establishment of the pan-Norwegian organisation *Østlandsk reising*. The Falk Committee appointed after the Torp Committee is dissolved when Professor Torp died in 1916.

1917   Major reform of both Riksmaal and Landsmaal.

1919   The 1917 language reform is accepted in Parliament by a small margin. This establishes the principle that Parliament has the final word in language planning matters. First novel translated from Norwegian Riksmål into Danish published.

1921   Halvdan Koht's *Working Class Uprising and Language Issues* (*Arbeidarreising og målspørsmål*) starts the process in the Labour Party of working towards its language planning policy of the 1930s.

1924   Conflict over oral language use in schools.

1925   The capital changes its name from Kristiania to Oslo.

1929   The names of the two written standards changed by Parliament from Riksmål and Landsmål to Bokmål and Nynorsk.

1930   Parliament decides that the city of Trondhjem will change its name to Nidaros. A fierce struggle follows. The city's current name, Trondheim, is then agreed by Parliament as a compromise. First Language Act passed by Parliament.

1933   Further discussions within the Labour Party about its language policy; Halvdan Koht's analysis and policy adopted.

1934   Appointment of a Language Committee to prepare a new language reform of both standards, with a clear pan-Norwegian mandate; Halvdan Koht appointed a member of the committee.

1938   Language reform of both standards passed by Parliament; the reform represents a radical sociolinguistic experiment.

1939   The 'Oslo decision': school textbooks in Oslo adopt the most radical Bokmål variety possible according to the 1938 reforms.

1940   Germany attacks and occupies Norway.

1941   The Nazi Government passes a language reform, which was obligatory for the media but was largely sabotaged in schools.

1944   The percentage of schoolchildren with Nynorsk as their main standard reaches its highest peak ever, 34.1 per cent.

1945   Liberation from the German occupation. The 1941 language reform nullified.

1948   Arnulf Øverland's *How Often Shall We Change Language?* (*Hvor ofte skal vi skifte sprog?*).

1949   Arnulf Øverland's *Bokmål – A Crippled Landsmål* (*Bokmålet – et avstumpet landsmål*).

1951   Parliament decides on a counting reform, the only official language planning decision ever taken in Norway concerning oral language forms.

1952   Establishment of an official and permanent Language Committee (*Norsk språknemnd*) with the mandate to continue work towards a pan-Norwegian solution. Launching of a private standard by the Riksmål movement.

1954   The 1939 'Oslo decision' suspended by the Oslo School Board after massive protest organised by 'The Parents' Campaign' against pan-Norwegian'.

1959   New textbook standard (*Ny læreboknormal*) decided on by Parliament.

1964	Sigurd Jahr Smebye wins court case about the use of upper-middle-class word forms in radio weather forecasts transmitted by the Norwegian Broadcasting Corporation. 'Language Peace Commission' appointed shortly afterwards.
1966	Recommendations of the 'Language Peace Commission'.
1972	The Language Committee discontinued and The Language Council established. The 'Liberation Resolution'. First referendum about joining the European Community, with 54 per cent voting 'no'.
1980	New Language Act passed by Parliament.
1981	Reform of Bokmål.
1992	The Sami language is recognised as an official language in some municipalities in northern Norway.
1994	Second referendum about joining the EU, 52 per cent voted 'no'.
2002	Parliament abandons the pan-Norwegian language planning policy.
2005	Reform of Bokmål.
2012	Reform of Nynorsk.
2013	Government decides to name 2013 'The Language Year', among other things to mark the 200th anniversary of the birth of Ivar Aasen.
2014	The 200th anniversary of the Norwegian Constitution.

Index

Page numbers in *italic* refer to illustrations.